COOL CAREERS WITHOUT COLLEGE FOR

WEB

SURFERS

COOL CAREERS WITHOUT COLLEGE FOR
WEB
SURFERS

**TONYA
BUELL**

The Rosen Publishing Group, Inc.
New York

Published in 2002, 2006 by The Rosen Publishing Group, Inc.
29 East 21st Street, New York, NY 10010

Library of Congress Cataloging-in-Publication Data

Buell, Tonya.
Cool careers without college for Web surfers / Tonya Buell.—1st ed.
  p. cm. — (Cool careers without college)
Includes bibliographical references and index.
Summary: Describes fourteen careers not requiring a college degree for people who are interested in computers, including job descriptions, education and training requirements, salary averages, career outlook, and a directory of where to go for more information.
ISBN-10 1-4042-1092-X
ISBN-13 978-1-4042-1092-9
1. Computer science—Vocational guidance—Juvenile literature.
[1. Computer science—Vocational guidance. 2. Vocational guidance.]
I. Title. II. Series.
QA76.25 .B82 2002
004'.023—dc21

2001003822

Manufactured in the United States of America

CONTENTS

INTRODUCTION

It is never too early to start thinking about your future career. The happiest employees are people who can say that they get to do what they love for a living. So, what do you love, and what sort of careers are associated with your passion?

When you get home from school, do you go straight to your computer? Do you spend hours at the community center working and playing on computers? Do you think about computers while doing other things? The world of the internet offers a wide variety of work to someone interested in computers and the web. This is a book for someone who enjoys working with computers, surfing the Internet, finding information on Web sites, and communicating with friends and associates through e-mail or blogs. You may even love video games and computer programs so much that you think about ways to make them better or more user-friendly. If that person is you, then you've picked the right career book.

There are many different types of jobs available for those interested in computers and the Internet, and—contrary to popular belief—many of those jobs do not require a college degree. Depending on what you like most, you can narrow down your career choices. For example, if you love everything about the Internet, you could be a Webmaster. If you are constantly engrossed in the latest video game, check out the chapter on becoming a game tester. If you're a do-it-yourselfer who is resourceful and courageous, you may want to become a Web entrepreneur.

The careers listed in this book don't require a college degree. Training, previous experience, and classes always help, so each chapter provides information on how to become the best career candidate possible—without having a degree. Get started now, and get prepared for success in your future!

1

GREETING THE WORLD FROM YOUR SCREEN: ONLINE COMMUNITY HOST

Do you find that you're so enthusiastic about a subject that you often tell others about it? Do you enjoy sharing information about issues or subjects near and dear to you? Do you research those issues or topics so that you are up-to-date on the latest news? If so, you may be a perfect candidate for online community hosting. Online community hosts provide information and articles about a particular subject over the Internet. They manage and provide opportunities for online discussions by their online community. Each host's community consists of people who specifically visit that Web site in order to learn and share knowledge about a particular subject. For example, a person may have gone on a diet, and lost a lot of weight. He or she may then start an online community for people hoping to lose weight. People who eventually surf that site may like what they see and decide to visit it often. They may even share their own stories of success or struggle with weight loss.

Online community hosts must have a sincere interest in their topic. They spend their days researching, writing about, and discussing that subject. They may review items or products related to their topic. Many online hosts also provide links to other Web sites. This means that they spend a lot of time surfing the Web for the best sites related to their subject.

People skills are a must-have for online hosts. They receive numerous e-mails from community members with questions, suggestions, and opinions. You will need to be informative, while also being supportive, even when receiving criticism. Now, that's a challenge! Online community hosts must also have strong writing skills. You'll need to write about your subject in a clear, informative, and interesting way.

Hosts should be very familiar with the Internet and the basics of creating Web pages. They should be able to

Because they operate in cyberspace, online community hosts can perform their jobs almost anywhere.

respond to their users' questions and suggestions quickly and efficiently. They should be able to come up with new and interesting content for their site weekly if not daily.

Online community hosts often work independently. They can work from wherever they can access their site, be it a community center, office space, or home.

Paying Your Dues

The most successful online hosts know as much as possible about their subjects. Read books, take classes, and do

online research to learn anything and everything about your subject.

Your other challenge is knowing how to build a Web site for your community, and how to maintain it. You can learn what is involved by surfing the Web. Start by reviewing sites that explain how the Web works, and what you need to create a Web site. Also, learn about Web software and skills. See if your school, local library, or community center offers classes or demos on Web building. If you know someone who has their own online community, ask if you can observe a typical day's work as a host (Make sure it's okay with your parents or guardians first.).

Earning a Living

An online host's salary varies greatly depending on many factors. If a site is popular, companies will want to advertise on it. This can mean big money, and a large salary. Some sites receive funds from community members. The funds cover operating costs, and may provide a small salary. Some hosts work for themselves while others work for companies with products or services for sale.

Often, an independent online host will have a second job at first, until his or her site begins to generate enough revenue to pay a reasonable salary. If the site becomes popular, he or she can earn up to $100,000 or more per year. Pay can be weekly, bi-weekly, or monthly.

Where It Is Headed

The Internet is increasingly becoming the place where people turn to for information. Online communities offer in-depth coverage and discussions that people searching for information need. Several companies and Web sites already employ online community hosts to bring their sites to life. Several of the large Web directories are employing these online hosts to provide the content, information, and links throughout their vast Web sites.

This is an ideal career for young people with a lot of energy, new ideas, and excitement about a specific topic. Like many Internet-related careers, the outlook for online community hosts is very bright.

Being an Online Community Host: The Pros and Cons of an Online Life

The best thing about being an online community host is that you get to spend most of your time working with a subject you really enjoy. For example, someone who hosts a community about computer games spends a large part of his or her time playing games in order to review them for the community. Someone

This host of an online book community is surrounded by several stacks of books that she plans to review for her site.

who hosts a community about books gets to read a lot of books. Someone who hosts a community about makeup gets to sample products. He or she contacts companies for new product information and samples regularly.

The con of hosting a Web site is that it is time-intensive. Online hosts often work every day of the week. The larger the site, the more information that must be kept current and accurate; the host is responsible for this. It's basically a project that never ends.

FOR MORE INFORMATION

WEB SITES

Build Your Own Web site
http://build-website.com
This Web site provides instructions and tips on building your own Web site.

HTML: An Interactive Tutorial for Beginners
http://html.about.com/index.htm?once=true&
This Web site is an online tutorial on HTML, the computer language used in creating and maintaining Web sites.

The Online Community Report
http://www.onlinecommunityreport.com
The Online Community Report provides information and articles about being an online community host. It also lists current job listings for online community hosts.

Web Style Guide
http://info.med.yale.edu/caim/manual
The Web Style Guide is a complete online style manual with information on interface, site and page design, graphics, multimedia, and animation.

BOOKS

Castro, Elizabeth. *HTML 4 for the World Wide Web Visual Quickstart Guide*. Berkeley, CA: Peachpit Press, 2000.
This book teaches the reader HTML, cascading style sheets, some JavaScript actions, and basic tips and techniques for creating Web pages.

Kilian, Crawford. *Writing for the Web*. Bellingham, WA: Self Counsel Press, 2000.
This book describes how to write for your target audience and develop content that works well online and communicates effectively.

Kim, Amy Jo. *Community Building on the Web: Secret Strategies for Successful Online Communities*. Berkeley, CA: Peachpit Press, 2000.
This book discusses how to build Web sites for a specific group of people, bring those people to the Web site, and motivate them to return.

Powazek, Derek M. *Design for Community: The Art of Connecting Real People in Virtual Places*. Berkeley, CA: New Riders Press, 2001.
This book explains how to host an online community. Each chapter offers interviews with hosts and experts.

Stefanov,Stoyan and Jeremy Rogers, Mike Lothar. *Building Online Communities with Phpbb 2: A Practical Guide to Creating and Maintaining Online Discussion Forums with Phpbb, the Leading Free Open Source Php/Mysql-Based Bulletin Board*. Birmingham, UK: Pakt Publishing, 2005.
This book discusses how to use a popular hosting application for an online community.

Werry, Chris, and Miranda Mowbray, eds. *Online Communities: Commerce, Community Action, and the Virtual University*. Upper Saddle River, NJ: Prentice Hall, 2001.
This book examines online communities: how they start, grow, and change, and what participants expect to gain when joining an online community.

Young, Margaret Levine, and John R. Levine. *Poor Richard's Building Online Communities: Create a Web Community for Your Business, Club, Association, or Family*. Lakewood, CO: Top Floor Publishing, 2000. This book provides basic information on how to build an online community for your club or group, as well as information on how to make online communities work, profit, and grow.

2

BINARY AND LITERARY LIFE: WRITER

Do you love the challenge of finding just the right word to express how you're feeling? Do you love to find well-written passages when you're reading a book or journal? Could you spend hours writing about your experiences or favorite subject? If so, then you may want to consider becoming a writer. Careers in writing come in many forms: You may write marketing brochures for a new company, develop the content for a Web site, or write a technical manual for a new technology or piece of equipment. Writers usually pick a favorite genre, such as fictional writing, nonfiction, or biographical writing and stick with it. They also choose the audience they'd like to write for; children, young adults, adults, or the general public.

Writers frequently do a large part of their research on the Internet. As a writer, you'll spend time surfing Web sites to collect information for your projects. You may also check to see how others have written articles or books about a similar topic. Writers spend their time researching content and becoming familiar with their subject matter, then they write original content about that subject, and edit what they've written. Writers need to know how to find the right words to communicate ideas. They need to understand the rules of grammar, and be able to write in a way that is interesting and understandable.

Writers must be able to pick a subject, deeply research it, and present the information as if they are an expert. If you understand computers and technical concepts very well, you may want to become a technical writer. If you are able to write material that is fun and persuasive, you may want to become a copywriter who writes content for Web sites. Candidates with an understanding of business or finance can become business and financial writers.

A freelance writer works in his home office.

Writers either work for companies as staff writers or they work as freelancers. Some companies may only need a writer for one specific project, while others have ongoing writing projects. Writers will often be working on more than one project at a time. They may have more than one client at a time. Many freelance writers work from home. They must have the discipline that is necessary to motivate themselves. They must understand their budget, and know how many projects they must take on at one time. A writer must also be able to work alone, as he or she will spend many hours in front of a computer, day or night.

Paying Your Dues

You don't need a college degree to be a writer, but you will be competing against candidates who have degrees, so you need to start building a writing portfolio. If you like the idea of technical writing, you're going to need to build a portfolio that shows you understand the styles of technical writing, and commonly used terms. Each type of writing has many styles as well as terms. Start researching the world of writing on the Web. You can find hints, tips, rules, and peek into the life of every type of writer.

Writing classes at school or the community center will also help. Research the topics that you like, and practice writing about them. Reading books is also a writer's secret skill sharpener. When you read other authors, you learn how they express themselves, or use words to reach you. You can then apply these devices to your own writing and subjects. Writers need knowledge of basic word processing programs, such as Microsoft Word. Also, many libraries offer classes on how to research for information, this is a good idea for any budding writer.

Earning a Living

Freelance writers are paid a flat fee for each project, or are paid hourly. A freelancer's salary depends on how much work he or she can do or get. Flat fees range from 10¢ to 30¢ per word, and hourly rates range from $10 to $50 per

Since many authors receive royalties based on sales of their books, it is in their best interest to investigate the market and the competition.

hour. According to the U.S. Department of Labor, the average annual salary for a writer author is $42,790.

Writers may earn royalties. This is a percentage of each book or project that is sold. If many books are sold, the writer will make more in royalties. It is helpful to visit your local library or bookstore to see what there is a demand for, what's already been published, and what really sells.

Where It Is Headed

According to the U.S. Department of Labor, writing jobs are expected to increase ten to twenty percent over the next six years. There will always be a need for talented writers who can write in a clear and interesting manner. New opportunities for writers, such as technical writing or writing Web content, have broadened the field even further. These opportunities will grow as the Internet community grows and as new technologies and tools arise. The public turns to the Internet and the writers who populate it with information.

Finding Your Beat: The Budding Writer

- Learn about subjects and try to explain them in your own words.
- Read books that have the type of writing that you like, such as fiction, nonfiction, feature, or biographical.
- Try to write for your school or town newspaper.
- Develop samples of your work by writing short articles or manuals about your preferred subject matter.
- Increase your vocabulary by learning one new word each day. Try to use each new word in your writing.

FOR MORE INFORMATION

ASSOCIATIONS

National Writers Union
113 University Place, 6th Floor
New York, NY 10003
(212) 254-0279
Web site: http://www.nwu.org
The National Writers Union is a union for freelance writers working in the United States.

WEB SITES

e-write.com
http://www.ewriteonline.com/
This site offers courses as well as links to many articles about writing for online readers.

Freelance Writers Site
http://freelancewrite.about.com
This Web site provides links and articles for freelance writers, as well as information on how to get freelance writing jobs.

Sun Microsystems: Writing for the Web
http://www.sun.com/980713/webwriting
This is an online book and guide that teaches you how to improve your Web writing skills.

Writers' Exchange Site
http://writerexchange.about.com
The Writers' Exchange site provides links and useful information for all types of writers, including articles and tips on writing, information on how to get writing jobs, and more.

Writer's Resource Center

http://www.poewar.com

This Web site contains numerous articles and links for all types of writers and provides online resources for writers.

BOOKS

Aslett, Don, and Carol Cartaino. *Get Organized, Get Published! 225 Ways to Make Time for Success*. Cincinnati, OH: Writers Digest Books, 2001.

This time-management book for writers describes many of the time management and organization issues that writers face, and provides 225 tips on making better use of your time.

Harris, Suzanne. *Writers' Wonderful Web*. Frederick, MD: Publish America, 2005.

This is a general reference book for writers, who use computers and the Web.

Kilian, Crawford. *Writing for the Web*. Bellingham, WA: Self Counsel Press, 2000.

Describes how to write for your target audience and develop content that works well online and communicates effectively.

Kipfer, Barbara Ann. *Writer's Digest Flip Dictionary*. Cincinnati, OH: Writers Digest Books, 2000.

This reverse dictionary helps you find the word that you're looking for when all you know is the definition.

Kovach, Bill, and Tom Rosenstiel. *The Elements of Journalism: What Newspeople Should Know and the Public Should Expect*. New York: Crown Publishers, 2001.

This book provides an in-depth look at the world of journalism today.

Marshall, Evan. *The Marshall Plan Workbook: Writing Your Novel from Start to Finish*. Cincinnati, OH: Writers Digest Books, 2001.

This workbook aids in the process of building characters, developing plot, and setting goals. It also provides plenty of marketing information and advice for writers.

Masello, Robert. *Writer Tells All: Insider Secrets to Getting Your Book Published*. New York: Henry Holt, 2001.
This book provides an enthusiastic look at the issues writers face, such as getting an agent, working with an editor, and promoting and selling a book.

Pringle, Alan S., and Sarah S. O'Keefe. *Technical Writing 101: A Real-World Guide to Planning and Writing Technical Documentation*.
Research Triangle Park, NC: Scriptorium Press, 2001.
This book describes the skills necessary to become a technical writer and explains the entire process of technical documentation.

Sammons, Martha C., and Sarah S. O'Keefe. The Internet Writer's Handbook. New York: Longman, 2003.
This book instructs online writers how to write well, with added information on HTML and Web formatting.

PERIODICALS
Publisher's Weekly
Web site: http://www.publishersweekly.com
This is the international news magazine of book publishing and bookselling.
Writer's Digest
Web site: http://www.writersdigest.com
This is the largest writer's magazine in the United States, featuring articles, tips, and writing competitions.

3

NOT THE NORMAL NEWS: BLOGGER

Do you keep a journal, or keep track of your days with an album or drawings? Do people often tell you that you're interesting, puzzling, or funny? Do you like sharing your opinions or bits of information with others? The online blog combines all of these elements into one career: the blogger. Blogging has taken the traditional journal into the twenty-first century. Thousands of people are turning to the Internet to publish their own kind of story. You could be one of them, and you could get paid.

The word blog is short for Weblog. A log, in this sense (and in the traditional sense), is a list of entries or details. A blog is a Web site that is updated daily or quite frequently. The kinds of entries or details depend entirely upon the owner or operator of the blog. The entries can be written words, articles, photographs, links to other sites or anything else. New items are entered and read at the top of the page, and older items move toward the bottom.

Blogs started out as personal pages, where someone entered material that was of specific interest to—or about—him or herself. This creates a really personal feel, where surfers can get a deep and up-close sense about the blog's owner. Blogs have grown to be included in big business, education, and government. Web publishers have several blogs run by different bloggers. Many of these types of blogs have ads from other businesses that bought advertising space on the Web site. E-commerce and information services have also adopted the blog format because surfers like the feeling of getting information from a "real" person. Political groups use blogs as a way to describe their views or actions in a very personal and immediate way.

Bloggers need to be good writers and researchers. If his or her blog is news-oriented, he or she needs to scour

Karl-Tohmas Musselman—age 19—writes for two Democratic blogs. Here, he uploads information while at a Boston pizzeria.

sources for the next big news item. Bloggers need to know how to write in a fun and interesting way so that people will read and visit the site. Many bloggers have repeat readers, who check the blog every day.

Paying Your Dues

You don't need a college degree to be an online blogger, but you must be able write in an interesting and thoughtful way. A commitment to producing new content every day is very important in maintaining readers and support.

Blogger Wanted: What the Ads Say

Blogging has become the next big thing, and companies are looking for the next big blogger. Following are examples of actual blogger wanted ads:

Blogger/copywriter/editorial-content producer

"Create, maintain and promote a blog that covers and reports about mobile-phone content and the marketplace. Must have experience creating and updating blogs, including creating links to other topical blogs. Blog savvy is a must. Salary 50-70K depending on experience."

Blog Correspondent

"We are currently looking for passionate sport/activity/location blog correspondents to join our editorial staff. Successful applicants should be able to write effectively and also have a deep passion/strong knowledge-base for their activity. Applicants should be witty and have a knack for finding good stories and blogging them. Post a minimum of 4 blog entries per day.

Pay based on an ad-revenue share system or contract. The more popular your blog and the more effort you put into it, the more money you make."

Blogging is a job that—as long as you have access to your browser or blog software—you can do from anywhere in the world.

Originally, a blogger needed to be computer and Web savvy. Currently, there are a number of software applications that allow a person to post entries to their blogs by a click of a button. This means bloggers don't necessarily need to know HTML. Some of these applications build the Web site for the user, so the user avoids having to know graphic design or Web development. If you do know these things, however, it will make you more desirable when it comes to salaried blog positions.

Many journalists are now turning to the blog format, This means that you may be competing with them for positions at companies. Taking classes or workshops on writing and communicating is a good idea. You'll also need to demonstrate that you can work as a blogger. If you have the resources available to you, create and maintain your own personal online blog as a test for yourself and a sample for potential employers.

Earning a Living

Blog salaries vary widely. Some personal blogs are actually supported by the people who read them. They send in funds to cover operating costs and to help the blogger maintain a living. Some blogs ask for subscription and advertising fees. Parts of these fees cover salaries. Other bloggers are salaried employees. According to the Wall Street Journal, the annual salary for this position ranges between $40,000 and $70,000 per year.

Where It Is Headed

According to the Wall Street Journal, only four percent of major U.S. corporations have blogs. This doesn't mean that the blogging future is bleak. On the contrary, Career Builder Inc's spokesperson, Jennifer Sullivan, says "Blogging jobs are growing in popularity." Companies are just now realizing that the natural, informal tone of a blog is the best way to sell products through the Internet. So long as there is a surfing public turning toward the Web for information, there will be a need for savvy, original, and dedicated online bloggers.

FOR MORE INFORMATION

ASSOCIATIONS

American Marketing Association://Blogs//
311 South Wacker Drive, Suite 5800
Chicago, IL 60606
(800) AMA-1150
Web site: http://marketingpower.blogs.com/american_
   marketing_associ/

This is a blog about blogs. It informs interested individuals in the use of blogs for advertising.

International Association of Online Communicators (IAOC)
37 Bozorth Hall, Rowan University
201 Mullica Hill Road
Glassboro, NJ 08028
Web site: http://www.onlinecommunicators.org
IAOC represents online communicators. According to its Web site, it "is dedicated to promoting and preserving the open and free communication that has been the foundation of the Internet community."

Media Bloggers Association (MBA)
(914) 325-4616
info-at-mediabloggers.org
Web site: http://www.mediabloggers.org
According to the Web site, "Media Bloggers Association (MBA) is a non-partisan organization dedicated to promoting MBA members and their blogs, educating bloggers, and promoting the explosion of citizen's media."

WEB SITES AND BLOG TOOLS

About, Inc: Weblog
http://weblogs.about.com/
This Web site explains blogging in-depth, and has tips for writing your first blog.

Bloggers Blog
http://www.bloggersblog.com
This Web site is by Writers Write, Inc. It "reports on blogging news and trends."

Build Your Own Web site
http://www.build-website.com
This is a useful and free tool for anyone wanting to learn how to build a Web site from scratch.

CBS News: How to Build a Blog
http://www.cbsnews.com/stories/2004/05/19/scitech/pcanswer/main618283.shtml
CBS News has a PC Answers section.. This article explains how to build a blog.

Dummies.com: Writing a Good Blog
http://www.dummies.com/WileyCDA/DummiesArticle/id-2848.html
This Web site is from the makers of the Dummies book series. This site tells you how to write on blogs.

MSDN: Blogging from Scratch
http://msdn.microsoft.com/msdnmag/issues/03/10/Blogging/default.aspx
For more advanced students, this site instructs people how to build a blog application from scratch.

Popular Science: How 2.0 "How to Build a Blog"
http://www.popsci.com/popsci/how2/article/0,20967,1051259,00.html
This site, part of Popular Science Magazine, directs you to inexpensive blogging tools.

Web Style Guide
http://info.med.yale.edu/caim/manual
The Web Style Guide is a complete online style manual with information on interface, site and page design, graphics, multimedia, and animation.

BOOKS

Bausch, Paul and Meg Hourihan, Mattew Haughey. *We Blog: Publishing Online with Weblogs*. Hoboken, New Jersey: John Wiley & Sons, Incorporated, 2002.
This blog book covers the history, as well as offers information on setting up and promoting your blog.

Blood, Rebecca. *Weblog Handbook: Practical Advice on Creating and Maintaining Your Blog*. New York, NY: Perseus Publishing, 2002.
This book covers the history of blogs, and has interviews with blog personalities. It also gives instructions on how to build a blog.

Doctorow, Cory and Shelley Powers, J. Scott Johnson, Rael Dornfest, Benjamin Trott. *Essential Blogging*. Sebastopol, CA: O'Reilly Media, Incorporated, 2002.
This book features several authors, who are leading bloggers, sharing stories and tips on blogging.

Gardner, Susannah and Xeni Jardin. *Buzz Marketing with Blogs For Dummies*. Hoboken, New Jersey: John Wiley & Sons, Incorporated, 2005.
This guide describes what blogging is and instructs you on how to set up a blog.

Gosney, John. *Blogging for Teens*. Boston, MA: Course Technology, Inc., 2004.
This book helps you decide what you want your blog to be about and offers instruction on how to build it.

Stone, Biz (Foreword by Wil Wheaton). *Who Let the Blogs out?: A Hyperconnected Peek at the World of Weblogs*. New York, NY: St. Martin's Press, 2004.
This book offers a lighthearted look at blogging, with stories and tips.

4

ALL AT YOUR FINGERTIPS: WEBMASTER

You've been given the whole project, and you're ready to go. You have design ideas, content to write, and the coolest tricks available to a Web builder. You negotiate your fee, and you set to work at creating a Web site for your latest client. Such is the life of a Webmaster and if it sounds like fun, this chapter is for you. A Webmaster is really the jack-of-all-trades of the Internet. He or she knows a little or a lot about just about everything. The Webmaster has the curiosity and ability to find out or learn about the few things he or she doesn't know.

Webmasters design, build, and maintain Web sites for companies. They must be familiar with Web design and development and have knowledge of graphic design and programming. They also need the technical skills and knowledge to place the sites on the World Wide Web, either through the companies' computers or through hosting companies. They also need to make sure that the sites are available to Web surfers and customers at all times.

Once a Web site is created and is put on the World Wide Web, a Webmaster monitors the site to determine the number of users who access the site. He or she may make changes or additions to the Web site on a regular basis. Making sure the site is secure from hackers is an important duty as well.

A Webmaster often works for a small or traditional company that wants to have a high-quality Web site but does not do all of its business over the Internet, and therefore does not need an entire team of programmers, designers, and developers. Many Webmasters work as freelancers. They create and maintain sites for several different companies. Therefore, in addition to the many qualities already listed, a Webmaster must have the ability to sell his or her services to a number of different small companies. He or she should be able to explain style ideas and elements to someone who might not know anything about the Web. This means patient and persuasive people skills.

Paying Your Dues

You don't need a college degree to be a Webmaster, but you do have to know the Web. Webmasters must be knowledgeable about almost every aspect of the Internet. They do most of their learning on the job. Things don't always go as expected, and a Webmaster must know how to fix things quickly, even if he or she doesn't have all the answers. Many Webmasters start out small, creating and maintaining simple Web sites, and teach themselves more as they work. Eventually, they become Internet experts.

If you have created a Web site for a school club or your family, you are already a Webmaster. Learn all you can about creating effective, professional-looking Web sites. You'll also need to learn about networks and Web hosting options. Read books about the Web and Internet.

Webmasters also need portfolios to show that they know how to design and maintain Web sites. You can build your portfolio by building Web sites for your friends, family, or anyone you know who needs a Web site. Your first several sites may be free of charge or for a very low fee, but eventually you will be able to charge a reasonable rate for your services.

Earning a Living

According to the U.S. Department of Labor, the average salary for Webmasters is $55,480. The early years of a Webmaster's career are all about building a portfolio, which means a low income. After you develop your skills and experience, you can expect to earn between $45,500 and $65,750 per year.

Outlook for the Future

Although there are many Webmasters currently in the job market, this field is a large and growing one. According to the U.S. Department of Labor, employment opportunities in Internet technologies are expected to increase thirty-six percent over the next six years. The Internet is reaching more people every day. Even small businesses are turning to the Internet to produce big profits. This means that any Webmaster candidate has a chance at landing clients. All it takes is know-how, drive, creativity, and a love for the Web. Therefore, those who choose Webmaster as a career should expect to have a solid future.

This mother and daughter cleaning business is a perfect example of a small business that could use the services of a Webmaster.

In the Paper: Webmaster Want-ad

Many companies that are hiring expect various skills from Webmaster candidates. There are a lot of different applications, programs, and Web technologies to learn in order to be employable. Here is a sample job description for a Webmaster:

HELP WANTED: WEBMASTER

Webmaster needed to design and develop Web applications. Must have experience with Microsoft Internet Information Server, Microsoft Application Server, firewalls, and routers. Experience with HTML, VBScript, JavaScript, Active Server Pages, SQL Server 7, and databases. Knowledge of Internet security protocols and Secure Socket Layer (SSL) helpful.

FOR MORE INFORMATION

ASSOCIATIONS

International Webmasters Association (IWA)

119 E. Union Street, Suite #F
Pasadena, CA 91103
(626) 449-3709
Web site: http://iwanet.org/index.html
IWA is an organization for Webmasters. It works to "provide and foster professional advancement opportunities among individuals dedicated to or pursuing a Web career."

WEB SITES

321 Webmaster

http://www.321webmaster.com
This is an online resource for Webmasters. It offers "one of the largest directories of free Webmaster resources, free Web hosting, free Web site tools, and even free e-mail."

Build Your Own Web site

http://www.build-website.com
This is a useful and free tool for anyone wanting to learn how to build a Web site from scratch.

PageResource.com

http://www.pageresource.com
PageResource.com is a Web development tutorial and information site, with tutorials on several aspects of Web design and development, including HTML and JavaScript. This site also contains practical articles on Web design.

Web Developer's Journal
http://www.webdevelopersjournal.com
This site provides helpful articles about creating a Web site, plus tools to download.

Web Style Guide
http://info.med.yale.edu/caim/manual
The Web Style Guide is a complete online style manual with information on interface, site and page design, graphics, multimedia, and animation.

BOOKS

Ditto, Christopher. *Webmaster Answers! Certified Tech Support*. Berkeley, CA: Osborne McGraw-Hill, 1998.
Common questions and answers for Webmasters, from developing Web sites to security and legal issues.

Douglas, Noel, Geert J. Strengholt, and Willem Velthoven. *Website Graphics Now*. New York: Thames & Hudson, 1999.
This book describes current and future developments in the world of graphic arts.

Holzschlag, Molly E. *HTML and CSS: The Smart Professional's Choice*. Upper Saddle River, NJ: Pearson Publishing, 2005.
This book shows Webmasters how to use HTML and CSS.

Maran, Ruth, and Maran Graphics. *Creating Web Pages with HTML Simplified*. 2nd Edition. Foster City, CA: IDG Books Worldwide, Inc., 1999.
This book is an easy-to-use guide to HTML and building Web pages. It is great for beginners and those wishing to learn how to build their own Web sites from scratch.

McCormack, Joe. *Webmaster's Guru Pack*. MnetWeb Services, 1999.
This book teaches Web development with the use of Perl and CGI. It also includes lots of screen shots, source code, and examples.

Niederst, Jennifer. *Web Design in a Nutshell: A Desktop Quick Reference, 3rd Edition*. Sebastopol, CA: O'Reilly & Associates, 2002.
This is a thorough reference, covering a number of different Web design topics, including HTML, graphics files, colors, multimedia, and style.

Spainhour, Stephen, and Robert Eckstein. *Webmaster in a Nutshell.* Sebastopol, CA: O'Reilly & Associates, 1999.
This book has information on just about every aspect of creating and maintaining a Web site: HTML, CGI, Perl, HTTP, server configuration, and Web administration.

Tauber, Daniel, and Brenda Kienan. *Webmastering for Dummies*. Foster City, CA: IDG Books Worldwide, Inc., 2001.
This is an easy-to-use guide on the basics of being a Webmaster.

Vaughn, Joan. *Webmaster Career Starter, 2nd Edition*. New York: Learning Express, 2001.
This book provides an overview of what it takes to become a Webmaster as well as information on how to get started in this career.

Williams, Robin, and John Tollett. *The Non-Designer's Web Book: An Easy Guide to Creating, Designing, and Posting Your Own Web Site*. Berkeley, CA: Peachpit Press, 2000.
A handy guide to building practical and attractive Web sites, for those who don't have professional Web design experience.

5

FINDING THE RIGHT FIT: TECHNICAL RECRUITER

The U.S. Department of Labor expects computer-related employment opportunities to increase thirty-six percent over the next six years. There are thousands of jobs to fill in the technical industry. Companies need help finding just the right employees to fill these positions. That's when the technical recruiter goes to work. A technical recruiter helps companies find the best employees for technical careers. Many companies hire technical recruiters to find the best employees and to convince potential employees to work for that company instead of for another company.

A technical recruiter is given the company's job openings. Then he or she posts the job ads on the Internet in order to reach job seekers. Many candidates post their resumés on the Internet. Recruiters scour the Internet looking for the most qualified. They then call or e-mail the individuals that they believe would be good for the job and schedule an interview.

Technical recruiters must have some technical knowledge themselves. They need to understand the skills that a company is asking an individual to possess. They will most likely interview the individual, and must be able to ask informed questions in order to gauge a potential employee's technical skills.

Even when the right candidate is found, the technical recruiter's job still isn't finished. The recruiter must convince the perfect candidate that he or she should accept the position over any other offers. This is because an individual may have several job offers from different companies and must decide which job to accept. A technical recruiter must be friendly, persuasive, and have the ability to negotiate.

Although companies with a large technical staff employ their own technical recruiters, many recruiters work for recruitment firms. Companies hire these firms to help them find the best employees for a variety of technical jobs. Often, recruiters not only search for the best employees but for the best jobs as well. Their goal is to match a quality individual with a quality job.

Paying Your Dues

You don't need a college degree to be a technical recruiter, but you do need drive, dedication, and the ability to find the right fit for employers and candidates. Technical recruiters work with computers, the Internet, and software such as Microsoft Office. You can take classes at your school or community center to help you get your computer skills in order. Technical recruiters must also have strong written communication skills. Take a communication or speech class as well as a business writing course.

Technical recruiters recruit for the technical industry, therefore they need to know about that industry. They need to know what they are asking from candidates in order to determine if that candidate has adequate experience. You can gain an understanding of basic technical terminology by taking a technical or computer class. In addition, periodically browse through the computer books and technical magazines at your local bookstore to see the latest technologies that are being used.

Raquel Garcia is a technical recruiter for Microsoft. Here, she attends a technical career fair to reach the best possible employee candidates. Microsoft expects to fill 7,000 tech jobs in 2006.

Earning a Living

According to the U.S. Department of Labor, the average salary for recruiters is $39,410. However, their salary can increase rapidly, especially if the recruiter is very talented. Many technical recruiters work on a commission basis, which means they receive a fee or percentage for each employee they place into a position. Skilled and experienced technical recruiters working on a commission basis can earn $100,000 per year or more.

Anyone considering a career as a technical recruiter should consider taking several basic computer courses.

Where It Is Headed

The demand for qualified technical employees is growing. According to the U.S. Department of Labor, the computer industry is expected to grow, which means jobs will always be in need of filling. Companies will need to turn to recruiters with proven skills to help sort through hundreds of possible employees. Candidates with skill in cutting edge technologies are highly desirable, and hard to find. Companies count on the speed and talent of recruiters to find those candidates and place them into employment with that company. Therefore, technical recruiters can expect to have a solid and steady future.

A Day in the Life: Technical Recruiter

Technical recruiters have very busy and varied schedules. Here is a sample of a day in the life of a typical technical recruiter:

Nathan works for a technical recruitment firm. He searches for the best candidates and offers them to companies with the best career options. His day starts bright and early, because he has an interview scheduled first thing in the morning. The interview goes well, but the candidate doesn't have the skills required for the job he had in mind. He doesn't give up on the candidate though, because she could be perfect for other job positions.

He has to put that on hold because the recruitment team has a meeting. They have a new client, who needs to hire forty

A technical recruiter and a candidate shake hands at the end of an interview.

technical personnel within the next six months. They will begin posting listings for each of the positions on the major career search sites. Nathan will also check his files for any candidates that might be qualified.

After the meeting, Nathan goes through his e-mail. He has a number of new resumés to look at, as well as e-mail replies from candidates he has interviewed. One candidate writes that he took another job instead of the one that Nathan had offered him. This means Nathan has to determine the next best candidate to fill the position he had hoped to fill with this candidate.

After Nathan finishes responding to his e-mails, he listens to his voice mail and returns phone calls. He then surfs the Web for new resumé postings. After lunch he has another two interviews with potential candidates.

FOR MORE INFORMATION

WEB SITES

Dice.com
http://www.dice.com
This is a job board for technology-related careers, where recruiters and employers can post available jobs and people can search for the perfect job.

HotJobs.com
http://www.hotjobs.com
HotJobs.com has many tools for recruiters and is a popular online job board.

Information on Web Searching
http://www.tesd.k12.pa.us/search/s-info.html
This is an online quick reference guide to eleven of the major search engines.

Recruiter's Network: Advanced Online Recruiting Techniques
http://www.recruiting-online.com/course52c.html
This is a large link-list of many recruiter sites and services.

BOOKS

Bolton, Robert. *People Skills.* New York: Simon & Schuster, 1986. This communication skills handbook shows how to get rid of common communication problems, resolve conflicts, and get what you want through effective communication.

Dawson, Charlie K. *The Complete Guide to Technical Recruiting.* Walnut Creek, CA: The Management Advantage, Inc., 1999. This is a practical guide for technical recruiters everywhere, with specific methods and checklists.

Dawson, Charlie K. *Internal Recruiter's Guide to Successful Technical Recruiting*. Walnut Creek, CA: The Management Advantage, Inc., 1999.
This book explains the basics of recruitment for a specific company and provides inspiration and technique for technical recruiters.

Ford, Wayne D., Ph.D. *Breakthrough Technical Recruiting*. Walnut Creek, CA: The Management Advantage, Inc., 2000.
This book explains how to find top technical people, how to convince employers to use your services, and how to negotiate successfully.

Graham, Donna M. *Online Recruiting: How to Use the Internet to Find Your Best Hire*. Palo Alto, CA: Davies-Black Publishing, 2000.
This step-by-step guide on how to recruit professionals over the Internet is useful for beginners as well as experienced recruiters.

Gralla, Preston. *How the Internet Works.* Indianapolis, IN: Que, 2001.
This book provides explanations and information about aspects of the Internet that most people find confusing, including explanations on Web browsers, e-mail, search engines, multimedia, and more.

Hughes, Rob and The Geek.com Staff. *Tech Speak: A Dictionary of Technology Terms Written by Geeks for Non-Geeks.* Boston, MA: Aspatore Books, 2003.
This is a dictionary of tech terms that any recruiter will need to know in order to be convincing and confident in the tech world.

Kador, John. *Internet Jobs! The Complete Guide to Finding the Hottest Internet Jobs.* New York: McGraw-Hill, 2000.
This book lists and describes the most popular and sought-after Internet jobs, provides information on the types of people and skills necessary for those jobs, and gives typical salary figures.

Mackie, Richard. *Take This Job and Sell It! The Recruiter's Handbook.* Fort Bragg, CA: QED Press, 1994.
This book teaches beginning recruiters the tactics and methods to success.

McKay, Matthew, Patrick Fanning, and Martha Davis. *Messages: The Communication Skills Book*. Oakland, CA: New Harbinger Publications, 1995.
Shows the reader how to master communication in his or her personal and professional life. A must for anyone in a service industry, as well as for those interested in enhancing their lives through communication.

Rothman, Johanna. *Hiring the Best Knowledge Workers, Techies & Nerds: The Secrets & Science of Hiring Technical People.* New York: Dorset House Publishing, 2004.
This book teaches recruiters how best to find and go after the right candidates for tech jobs.

Schoyen, Christian, and Nils Rasmussen. *Secrets of the Executive Search Experts*. New York: Amacom, 1999.
This book describes several important strategies and methods that successful recruiters use, and provides tips and an explanation of useful terms.

PERIODICALS

Fast Company
http://www.fastcompany.com
This magazine is full of new and innovative approaches to the business world.

6

HOW MAY I HELP YOU?: E-COMMERCE CUSTOMER SERVICE REPRESENTATIVE

Have you ever contacted someone for help about the Web? That person—the e-commerce customer service representative—listened to your issue and tried to help you resolve it. If you've often thought that you could be a great help to people seeking Web answers, you may want to become an e-commerce customer service representative.

Large e-commerce companies employ customer service representatives to guide their users through their Web sites. They answer the users' questions about services and products, and to assist customers in resolving problems. These representatives must be friendly, Web-savvy, patient, and willing to help others.

Many customer service representatives work over the telephone, via e-mail, and through online chatting to communicate with their customers. Many customers may be stressed or annoyed at problems that they encountered. A representative must understand this, and communicate with the customer in a calm, clear way. Representatives do not use slang, curse words, or unprofessional language because they are representing their company, not themselves. A representative can expect to handle many telephone calls and e-mails per day, and therefore must love communicating with others.

E-commerce customer service representatives must be very familiar with their company's services and products since they'll be guiding customers to either maintain or purchase them. Most companies will have a specific set of guidelines for their customer service representatives, with detailed instructions for how to respond to any question a customer asks. However, they often receive questions that are new or unexpected. The representative should be able to answer questions quickly and efficiently.

E-commerce customer service representatives are often available by both telephone and e-mail.

He or she must know when to direct the difficult questions to a supervisor.

E-commerce customer service representatives must be familiar with the Internet, e-mail, and their company's Web site. They may need to guide a user around it. He or she will demonstrate to a user how to search for services or products. An e-commerce customer representative may actually have to teach the customer certain Web surfing techniques while on the phone. If a customer has a problem, but doesn't use the proper terminology, a representative must be able to get a sense of what the customer is trying to communicate. He or she must then fix the problem while being sensitive to the customer's need for help.

Paying Your Dues

To be a representative, you'll need to the know the Internet, but you won't need a college degree. Read books on the basics of the Internet to learn how Web sites work, what "cookies" do, and the best ways to use a search engine. Surf the Web to determine what tools and information are available online and teach yourself how to use e-mail soft-ware such as Outlook or Eudora. Knowing the basics of the Internet will bring you one step closer to getting an e-commerce customer service position.

An e-commerce customer service representative must be friendly, able to communicate well, and able to handle customer complaints. Writing and speech classes will help you hone your communication skills. You can also start on your career path by getting a customer service job after school or on the weekends. Retail stores have customer service positions that can give you experience and help to build your resumé. You'll learn the delicate balance of being resourceful, tactful, and helpful, all at the same time.

Earning a Living

According to the U.S. Department of Labor, customer service representatives usually earn between $20,960 and $33,540

After-school jobs at retail stores are often good training grounds for customer service representatives.

per year. Computer help-desk support staff earn between $27,500 to $56,500 per year. Pay varies based on experience and skills. Some representatives may work on an hourly basis, earning between $10 and $17 per hour. Many companies have twenty-four-hour customer service, so representatives have their choice of shifts.

Experienced and ambitious customer service representatives can often work their way up into manager or supervisor positions. According to the U.S. Department of Labor, they earn between $29,960 and $50,660 per year.

Where It Is Headed

The amount of sales and services done over the Internet is growing rapidly and is expected to continue growing. The industry has a high-turnover, which means there are always opportunities available. This is because experienced representatives transfer to other positions. Young people take part-time hours, which leave full-time hours available. So long as there is e-commerce, there will be a need for customer service representatives.

E-commerce Q and A

A user contacts customer service via telephone or online. A representative responds quickly and clearly, in order to get to the heart of the matter. Here are some tips on answering user questions:

Determine what it is the customer is asking

Sometimes customers know what the problem is, but are not quite clear when communicating it. Speak clearly and ask questions to get to the heart of the issue. Don't correct the customer, but guide them so they know what to do next time by themselves.

Answer clearly and completely

The customer wants to hear "yes" or "no," not "maybe" or "I'm not sure." Make sure the answer is clear. If a customer hears a confident representative, he or she will relax and trust the information they are receiving.

Redirect any problems or difficult questions

If you don't know the answer to a question, or if the customer is angry or argumentative, transfer the customer to your supervisor immediately.

FOR MORE INFORMATION

ASSOCIATIONS

International Customer Service Association
401 North Michigan Avenue
Chicago, IL 60611
(800) 360-4272

Web site: http://www.icsa.com
This association works to aid, instruct, and bring together customer service professionals worldwide.

WEB SITES

Customer Service Job Store

http://www.customerservicejobstore.com
This Web site posts job openings that relate specifically to customer service.

Hotjobs.com

http://www.hotjobs.com
Hotjobs.com is a large Web site offering many jobs in customer service in many different geographical locations. The site allows you to post your resumé so that potential employers can find you.

Monster.com

http://www.monster.com
Monster.com is a popular job-search site for all types of careers. It's a great place to find e-commerce customer service careers.

Vault

http://www.thevault.com
Along with posting customer service jobs, Vault also offers several different services, such as resumé building, interviewing techniques, and salary information.

BOOKS

Anderson, Kristin and Ron Zemke. *Delivering Knock Your Socks Off Service*. New York: AMACOM, 2002.
This book explains how to provide top-notch customer service for online, telephone, and in-person customers.

Bolton, Robert. *People Skills*. New York: Simon & Schuster, 1986. This communication skills handbook shows how to get rid of common communication problems, resolve conflicts, and get what you want through effective communication.

Evenson, Renee. *Customer Service 101: Basic Lessons to Be Your Best*. Whitehouse Station, NJ: Bull's Eye Publishing, 1997.
This book clearly explains the basic rules for great customer service and is useful for anyone in the service industry.

Gralla, Preston. *How the Internet Works*. Indianapolis, IN: Que, 2001.
This book provides explanations and information about aspects of the Internet that most people find confusing, including explanations on Web browsers, e-mail, search engines, multimedia, and more.

Griffin, Jill. *Customer Loyalty: How to Earn It, How to Keep It*. Hoboken, New Jersey: John Wiley & Sons, Inc., 2002.
This book explains how customer loyalty and trust is built through strong customer service and other means.

Karr, Ron, and Don Blohowiak. *The Complete Idiot's Guide to Great Customer Service*. New York: Alpha Books, 1997.
This book shows how to develop a great customer service program, handle complaints, and more.

Kegan, Robert, and Lisa Laskow Lahey. *How the Way We Talk Can Change the Way We Work: Seven Languages for Transformation*. San Francisco: Jossey-Bass, 2001.
This book provides a revolutionary approach to communication in the workplace and shows what language is most effective when communicating with others.

Leland, Karen, and Keith Bailey. *Customer Service for Dummies*. Foster City, CA: IDG Books Worldwide, Inc., 1999.

This book provides information, inspiration, and practical advice for customer service representatives.

Levine, John R., Carol Baroudi, and Margaret Levine Young. *The Internet for Dummies*. Foster City, CA: IDG Books Worldwide, Inc., 2000.
This book provides clear, easy-to-understand explanations and advice for using the Internet. It includes information on how to pick an Internet service provider (ISP) and how to protect your privacy, as well as surfing, shopping, and e-mail.

McKay, Matthew, Patrick Fanning, and Martha Davis. *Messages: The Communication Skills Book*. Oakland, CA: New Harbinger Publications, 1995.
This book shows the reader how to master communication in his or her personal and professional life. It is a must-have for anyone in a service industry, as well as for those interested in enhancing their lives through communication.

Morgan, Rebecca L. *Calming Upset Customers*. Menlo Park, CA: Crisp Publications, 1996.
This popular book teaches what makes customers upset, how to determine what they want, and how to calm them down.

PERIODICALS

Fast Company
http://www.fastcompany.com
This magazine is full of new and innovative approaches to the business world.

7

MONEY TO BE MADE: WEB ENTREPRENEUR

Some ideas simply sell. They're good ideas, products, or services that people really want. Do you have good ideas? Do you like the idea of supplying and selling what the public wants, all on the Web? You may be a future Web entrepreneur in the making. Web entrepreneurs start their own businesses over the Internet. First, they determine what product or service to sell. Next, they come up with a plan of how they will make money selling that product or service. They must use their own personal savings or persuade others to invest money in their company. They hire a person or company to build their e-commerce Web site. They must also determine a marketing plan so that customers will know about and visit their Web site.

Once the Web site is online and accepting orders, Web entrepreneurs must continuously work to ensure that the business is making money. They also have to make sure that the customers are happy. They check to see what sells and what doesn't. The entrepreneur will concentrate on the money-makers. They may decide to raise or lower the prices of their products or enhance their marketing efforts so that the business is as profitable as possible.

Web entrepreneurs must be able to work independently. They need the ability to follow through with projects. Since they often risk their own time, ideas, and money in building the business, they must be able to take risks and make smart decisions. Web entrepreneurs must also be willing to work long or unusual hours, especially in the beginning.

Paying Your Dues

Most colleges do not offer degrees in Web entrepreneurship. Colleges do, however, offer degrees in business, and many business majors turn their attention to Internet enterprises.

This means you'll want to level the playing field by studying business. You'll also want to know about marketing, or how to reach the public and get them to buy whatever you're selling. Many community colleges or learning centers offer classes on starting your own business. Read books on the subject, too.

In addition, you must know as much as possible about the products or services you intend to sell. Surf the Web to determine your main competitors. Find out what prices they are charging, and what special services they offer. Do research on the audience that you want to reach. What do they like and how do they like to be persuaded? Gain valuable practice in starting your own business by mowing lawns, walking dogs for your neighbors, or cleaning houses and apartments in your area.

Earning a Living

The salary for a Web entrepreneur varies widely. Many entrepreneurs will lose money if their business is not a success. On the other hand, some successful entrepreneurs are able to make millions of dollars. After initial start-up costs, its important to keep expenses down in order to increase your profit margin.

When you decide to become a Web entrepreneur, you determine your salary by planning how much money you expect your business to make. Sometimes, you may have to

E-commerce businesses can be run from one room. Here, entrepreneurial partners discuss their start-up business.

work for free until your business becomes successful. You may need a part-time job while your company is new.

Where It Is Headed

The Internet is growing and changing at a rapid pace. This means that there is a continuous need for new products and services. At the same time, however, many large companies, such as Amazon.com, are becoming leaders in most of the traditional markets. It may become more difficult for your

Your Own Web Business: Things That You Need to Do

- Come up with a great idea of a product or service to sell. Base this idea on what you think people need or desire.
- Create a business plan: consider how you will sell it on your Web, how much it will cost to get started, how much money you expect to make, and so on.
- Research how similar businesses are doing.
- Hire someone to build your Web site, or build it yourself.
- Determine how orders will be shipped or services will be provided. Purchase an inventory, if necessary.
- Develop a marketing plan to bring customers to your Web site.
- Continuously reevaluate and redefine your business, with profits in mind.

business to compete with large, established Internet companies. In the future, the only way for your business to succeed may be to offer what the big companies don't. To find out what this is, a Web entrepreneur must continue researching the subject.

Starting your own business is one of the riskiest—and most rewarding—enterprises a person can do. Thousands of small businesses open each year, while thousands fold. The outlook for any new business is uncertain. If you are new at starting and running your own business, you may not know what obstacles to expect. Even though you may have done your research, the public can be unpredictable. As long as an entrepreneur has a back-up plan—and savings to fall back on as well—the outlook for entrepreneurship is wide open.

FOR MORE INFORMATION

ASSOCIATIONS

U.S. Small Business Administration
409 Third Street SW
Washington, DC 20416
(800) 827-5722
Web site: http://www.sba.gov
The U.S. Small Business Administration is a government organization that provides information, loans, and other resources for small businesses.

WEB SITES

CNN Financial Network
http://money.cnn.com
CNN Financial Network provides up-to-the-minute news on the markets; highlights companies, funds, and trading strategies; and features lots of tools, links, and resources useful for anyone in the business world.

Quicken Small Business Center
http://quicken.com/small_business
The Quicken Small Business Center provides information, news, and articles on starting your own business, and contains links to many different resources for small business owners.

Small Business Advisor
http://www.isquare.com
This Web site is filled with advice for starting and operating a small or home-based business, plus news, tips, and more.

Startup Journal—The Wall Street Journal Center for Entrepreneurs
http://startup.wsj.com
This Web site contains information, articles, and resources for those who want to start their own business.

Web Entrepreneurs at Berkeley
http://www.ocf.berkeley.edu/~web
This organization works to "facilitate learning, knowledge exchange and promote discussion of e-business opportunities among all members," and is open to students with Web knowledge.

BOOKS

Cannon, Jeff. *Make Your Website Work for You: How to Convert Online Content Into Profits*. New York: McGraw-Hill, 2000.
This book explains how to profit from your Web site, get customers to surf it, and develop successful marketing strategies.

Edwards, Paul, Sarah Edwards, and Linda Rohrbough. *Making Money in Cyberspace*. New York: J P Tarcher/Putnam, 1998.
This book explains how to start and run a successful online business, as well as how to bring your existing business online.

Gielgun, Ron E. *121 Internet Businesses You Can Start from Home: Plus a Beginners Guide to Starting a Business Online*. Brooklyn, NY: Actium Publishing, 1997.
This book has information on how to start and operate a business on the Internet, as well as a comprehensive list of 121 online businesses that can be started from home.

Holden, Greg. *Starting an Online Business for Dummies*. Foster City, CA: IDG Books Worldwide, Inc., 2000.
This book contains information on writing a business plan and getting financed, as well as technical tips and business strategies.

McKay, Matthew, Patrick Fanning, and Martha Davis. *Messages: The Communication Skills Book*. Oakland, CA: New Harbinger Publications, 1995.
This book shows the reader how to master communication in his or her professional life. It is a must-have for anyone in a service industry, as well as those interested in enhancing their lives through communication.

O'Neill, Julia K. and Hugo Barreca. *Entrepreneur's Internet Handbook: Your Legal and Practical Guide to Starting a Business Website*. Naperville, IL: Sourcebooks, Inc., 2002.
This book will give you an idea of the legal side to running an e-commerce business. It shows you contracts and important information that will help you establish a legally-sound business.

Powers, Mike. *How to Start a Business Website*. New York: Avon Books, 1999.
This book contains lots of practical information on starting your own online business, including how to convince customers to buy your

product, how to get noticed by search engines, and how to find new customers.

Reynolds, Janice. The Complete E-Commerce Book: Design, Build, and Maintain a Successful Web-based Business. Gilroy, CA: CMP Books, 2004.
This book teaches readers how to start an e-commerce company from the ground up.

Rich, Jason R. *The Unofficial Guide to Starting a Business Online*. Foster City, CA: IDG Books Worldwide, Inc., 1999.
This book provides step-by-step advice and information on starting a business online, from choosing the right business to creating an effective marketing plan.

PERIODICALS

Fast Company
http://www.fastcompany.com
This magazine is full of new and innovative approaches to the business world.

8

SURF'S UP!: WEB DESIGNER

Without Web sites, there would be nowhere to surf. Think about the thousands of sites on the Internet. Each one represents the person—or people—who built it. If you often think of different and better ways the Web sites could appear, a career in Web design may be for you. Web designers determine what pictures, animations, and logos will

75

appear on each Web page. They decide the formatting of the Web site, and how many pages it will be. They create the layout of the text, pictures, advertisements, and logos, and they decide what colors and fonts look best.

Web design is a creative job, since designers determine how the Web will look. Web design also requires business sense and marketing skills. Many Web pages serve as online brochures for companies. They must present the company's products or services in the most appealing way. This means that the Web site should look professional and express the attitude and goals of the company in an attractive way.

The Web designer's tools are the computer and Web-building software. They often create layouts for Web sites using a Web editor like FrontPage or Dreamweaver. They are familiar with HTML. This is the basic programming language for creating Web pages. They also need graphic design skills and should be able to use graphic design software like Photoshop, Illustrator, or Freehand. Web designers know a little—or a lot—about many different things!

Large-scale Web site projects involve a team of professionals. This includes graphic artists, animators, developers, and programmers. A Web designer should be able to get along well with others, and take direction well, too. The designer must be able to put great effort into a Web site, but be able to change it if the client or team wants something

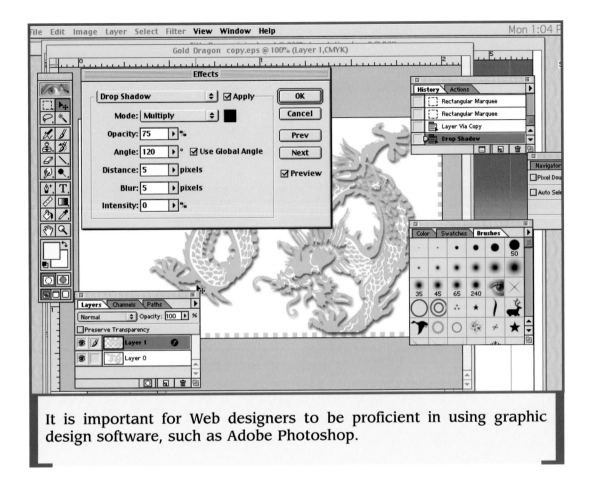

It is important for Web designers to be proficient in using graphic design software, such as Adobe Photoshop.

different. They also need to plan their work well so that the design is completed on time.

Paying Your Dues

There are college-level courses in Web design, so you'll want to obtain at least this level of knowledge on your own. Many Web designers do not have college degrees, but have excellent design sense and Web building-skills. You'll need a very comfortable ease with HTML and concepts of Web development. Check your local resources, such as schools

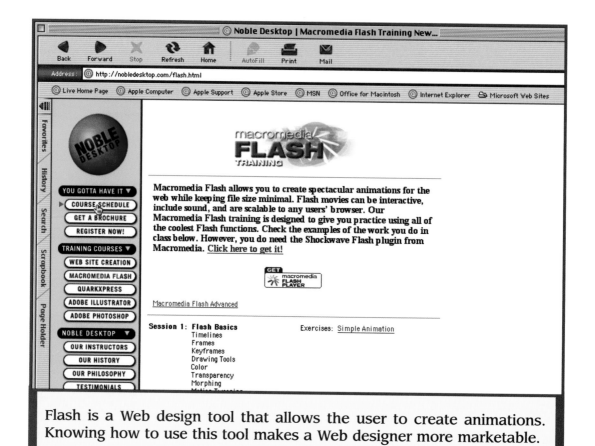

Flash is a Web design tool that allows the user to create animations. Knowing how to use this tool makes a Web designer more marketable.

and the community center for classes on Web building. You can also go online to gain a deeper understanding of Web design and development, as well as HTML. Taking classes in other Web development languages and tools, such as JavaScript or Flash, is also very helpful.

In order to be competitive, you'll also need graphic design skills. Even simple buttons that link your pages together are created using graphic design techniques. You can create them (as other designers do) using graphic software such as Photoshop or Illustrator.

In Web design, practice makes perfect. Practice creating attractive and appealing Web sites for family and friends, or create your own Web site with information about your favorite subjects. The more you practice, the more you'll become familiar with tools and techniques that designers use to make their sites look professional and high-tech.

Earning a Living

According to the U.S. Department of Labor, the annual salary for a Web designer averages between $51,250 to $73,750. Designers with a decent sample portfolio usually start at around $30,000. The salary for freelance Web designers varies based on what projects each freelancer takes on, and what he or she charges.

Where It Is Headed

According to the U.S. Department of Labor, employment in the computer industry is expected to grow thirty-six percent over the next six years. Opportunities abound, especially for Web designers. A search for Web design jobs in any of the large job search sites will produce hundreds of listings throughout the United States and the world.

Software and Computer Languages for Web Designers 101

Software:

Browsers such as Microsoft Internet Explorer and Netscape Communicator allow you to view how your Web site will appear to your users.

Web editors like Microsoft FrontPage and Macromedia Dreamweaver allow you to develop Web pages quickly and easily.

Graphic design software such as Adobe Photoshop and Macromedia Freehand allow you to create pictures, buttons, lines, and logos.

Animation tools like Flash and 3D Studio help you create animations and moving pictures.

Languages:

HTML, or hypertext markup language, is the basic programming language for Web sites.

JavaScript allows you to add simple programs to your Web site.

FOR MORE INFORMATION

ASSOCIATIONS

Guild of Accessible Web Designers (GAWD)
http://www.gawds.org
This guild is dedicated to making Web sites accessible to everyone, including people with impairments. Their "Site of the Month" section allows members to vote for which Web site they think has the most excellent design.

WEB SITES

Build Your Own Website
http://www.build-website.com
This useful and free tool is for anyone who wants to learn how to build a Web site from scratch.

CoolHomePages.com
http://www.coolhomepages.com
CoolHomePages.com is a Web site with links to hundreds of cool and attractive-looking sites, where designers can find inspiration and great ideas.

PageResource.com
http://www.pageresource.com
PageResource.com is a Web development tutorial and information site, with tutorials on several aspects of Web design and development, including HTML and JavaScript. This site also contains practical articles on Web design.

Web Design Group: HTML Help
http://www.htmlhelp.com/

This is an online reference designed to be nonspecific as to platforms, browsers, and applications. The hope is that anyone can use the information, whether they use Macs or PCs.

Web Developer's Journal
http://www.webdevelopersjournal.com
This online resource features articles of interest to anyone building a Web site, from first-timers to experienced designers.

Web Style Guide
http://info.med.yale.edu/caim/manual
The Web Style Guide is a complete online style manual with information on interface, site and page design, graphics, multimedia, and animation.

BOOKS

Anderson, Ruth Ann. *Exploring the Art and Technology of Web Design*. Florence, KY: Thomson Delmar Learning, 2005.
This book covers all the basics of Web design, and shows how to create visually appealing sites.

Krug, Steve. *Don't Make Me Think: A Common Sense Approach to the Web*. Berkeley, CA: New Riders, 2005.
This book presents Web design do's and don'ts.

Lynch, Patrick J., and Sarah Horton. *Web Style Guide: Basic Design Principles for Creating Web Sites*. New Haven, CT: Yale University Press, 1999.
This text presents all of the basics of designing a Web site, including page layout, graphics, and multimedia.

Maran, Ruth, and Maran Graphics. *Creating Web Pages With HTML Simplified*. 2nd ed. Foster City, CA: IDG Books Worldwide, Inc., 1999.
This book is an easy-to-use guide to HTML and building Web pages, great for beginners and those wishing to learn how to build their own Web sites from scratch.

Mumuawce, Stefan. *Simple Web Sites: Organizing Content-Rich Web Sites into Simple Structures.* Gloucester, MA: Rockport Publishers, 2005.
This book discusses how to make Web sites visually stunning yet simple, so they are easy and enjoyable to surf.

Stein, Bob. *Web Design Color Reference Card.* VisiBone, 2000.
This is a clear and logical reference card of colors for the World Wide Web.

Stein, Bob. *Web Designer's HTML Card Reference Guide.* VisiBone, 2000.
This is a quick-reference card with definitions and descriptions of nearly all HTML tags.

Williams, Robin, and John Tollett. *The Non-Designer's Web Book: An Easy Guide to Creating, Designing, and Posting Your Own Web Site.* Berkeley, CA: Peachpit Press, 2000.
This handy guide to building practical and attractive Web sites is geared to those who don't have professional Web design experience.

Ziegler, Kathleen, and Nick Greco. *The Designer's Guide to Web Type: Your Connection to the Best Fonts Online.* Cincinnati, OH: Writers Digest Books, 2001.
This book provides information on attractive and appealing fonts for use on Web sites.

9

BRINGING IT TO LIFE: ANIMATOR

Three people are playing a video game together. One is in California, one is in Florida, and the other is in Hawaii. These multi-user games—as well as single-user games—are animated by graphic animators. Traditionally, animators worked for companies such as Disney, but now animation has grown because of computers. Today's animator might

84

create graphic images for a popular video game. He or she might draw characters and pictures for an online animated short story. Graphic animators may produce the moving images and animations you see on the Web and your computer programs.

A few years ago, many animators drew characters using a pencil and sketch paper. Today, almost all of the current work is done electronically. Graphic animators do their work on a computer, using computer graphics and animation software. It is mandatory that animators are familiar with computers and the software that the industry uses.

Another recent change in the animation industry is the type of companies that need animators and the kinds of jobs that are available. Only recently, most animators worked for the big movie and television studios. Now, however, many animators work for dot-com companies, new media companies, and computer and video game manufacturers. Many animators also work for themselves. They freelance for different companies and work from home or their own office.

Animators must be creative and artistic. They need to be detail oriented, and have strong technical and computer skills. They should also possess good people skills. Animators often work on a team with other animators, programmers, artists, and developers. They must be able to take direction well. If the project manager doesn't like what he or she sees, the animator must change it.

Paying Your Dues

The first and foremost requirement of animation is drawing talent. If you're not confident in your abilities, take classes in art and drawing. You should be able to create characters and figures with pen and paper as well as on the computer. Any classes on character design and storyboarding will be extremely helpful as well.

Animators should also have a strong familiarity with computer animation tools such as Flash and 3D Studio. Check to see if your school or community center offers classes in graphic animation. You will also want to be familiar with graphic design software, such as Photoshop, Illustrator, and Freehand. Usually, it is possible to download free trial versions of software so you can try them. Also, check your school library resource center or community center for these applications.

To begin a career in animation, it is extremely important to have samples of your work. Employers will want to see samples of pen and paper drawings, as well as actual short computer animations. Use your imagination to create a short story or situation. Build the animated cartoon using

A computer animator creates character sketches on a drawing pad. It is important that computer animators know how to draw with pen and paper.

This scene is from the popular computer-animated movie *Antz*.

software such as Flash or 3D Studio. If you have a Web site, you can post your animation as an online portfolio.

Earning a Living

According to the U.S. Department of Labor, the average salary for mulit-media designers and animators is $43,980. Most animators earn between $33,970 and $61,120 per year. Extremely talented animators at large studios can make over $100,000 annually. Freelance animators have varying salaries, depending what they charge and accomplish.

Where It Is Headed

According to the U.S. Department of Labor, employment of artists (including animators) is expected to grow ten to twenty percent over the next six years. Various areas of animation are more stable than others. The computer game industry is always creating new games and updating old ones. The movie and entertainment industry is somewhat less predictable. Animation features are popular one year and not the next. Television is somewhat more consistent.

The Internet-based need for animators is consistent and growing. There is a very large need for animation in Internet advertisements and brochures. This is because competition for customers via the Web is fierce. Companies want interesting, eye-catching animations to lure customers. The more original and clever the animation, the better. People remember companies with well-designed sites.

Going Live Your First Time: Animation

In order to land your first job, you must be able to show employers samples of your work. The more that you have to show an employer, the better. So, how do you get started creating your first piece of animation? Follow these steps and you'll be on your way!

COOL CAREERS WITHOUT COLLEGE

1. Think of an idea for a short, simple cartoon.
2. Plan the characters and basic backgrounds for each scene.
3. Draw the characters and basic backgrounds using a design software like Photoshop or Freehand.
4. Bring life to the characters using animation software like Flash or 3D Studio. Make their eyes move around, their mouths open and close when they talk, and their feet and arms move when they walk.
5. Record voices or create subtitles using animation software.
6. Show your creation to your family and friends, as well as potential employers. If you have a Web site, post it there, and you've become an online animator!

FOR MORE INFORMATION

ASSOCIATIONS

International Game Developers Association
600 Harrison Street
San Francisco, CA 94107

(415) 947-6235
Web site: http://www.igda.org
The International Game Developers Association is a nonprofit organization for developers of games and entertainment software. Members receive free or discounted rates on publications, conferences, and software.

WEB SITES

Animation 101
http://library.thinkquest.org/25398
Animation 101 is a Web site that provides news, history, and tutorials on several major types of animation.

Animation Magazine
http://www.animationmagazine.net
This Web site is devoted to the "business, technology, and the art of animation." It asks for users to sign in for free access to articles.

Animation World Network
http://www.awn.com
Animation World Network provides news, articles, information, and job listings for animators worldwide.

GameJobs.com
http://www.gamejobs.com
This Web site is a job board for those looking for work in the computer game industry. It also offers tips, links, and resource materials.

Hotwired: Animation Express
http://hotwired.lycos.com/animation
This Web site has many innovative animations, grouped by animation type, plus resources, tools, and tutorials. It also gives users the ability to submit their animations for publication on the site.

BOOKS

Blatner, David, and Bruce Fraser. *Real World Photoshop 6*. Berkeley, CA: Peachpit Press, 2001.

This is a straightforward manual on using Photoshop 6, one of the most popular graphic arts tools.

Clarkson, Mark. *Flash 5 Cartooning*. Foster City, CA: IDG Books Worldwide, Inc., 2001.
This book explains how to use Flash 5 software to create cartoon animation. It contains lots of examples and advice for current and aspiring animators.

Culhane, Shamus. *Animation from Script to Screen*. New York: St. Martin's Press, 1990.
This book contains helpful information and exercises to get started in screen animation.

Delmar Learning Staff. *Game Development Essentials: Video Game Art*. Florence, KY: Thomson Delmar Learning, 2004.
This book explores the art of video games.

Douglas, Noel, Geert J. Strengholt, and Willem Velthoven. *Website Graphics Now: The Best of Global Site Design*. New York: Thames & Hudson, 1999.
This book describes current and future developments in the world of graphic arts.

Franklin, Derek, and Brooks Patton. *Flash 5! Creative Web Animation*. Berkeley, CA: Peachpit Press, 2001.
This book and CD package contains information about Flash 5, its latest features, and hundreds of tips and tricks explaining how to create animations with Flash 5.

Hart, Christopher. *Manga Mania Video Games: How to Draw the Characters, Fighting Poses, and Environments of Manga Style Video Games*. New York: Watson Guptill Publications, Inc., 2004.
This is a guide to illustrating in a video game style.

Mohler, James. *Flash 5.0: Graphics, Animation and Interactivity*. Albany, NY: Delmar Thomson Learning, 2000.

This straightforward guide to Flash 5 covers all of the latest features of Flash and offers practice exercises.

Myers, Dale K. *Computer Animation*. Milford, MI: Oak Cliff Press Inc., 1999.
This book describes careers in animation and helps the reader turn his or her interest in animation into a successful career.

Raugust, Karen. *The Animation Business Handbook*. New York: St. Matin's Press, 2004.
This book delves into the business side of animation, from idea to screen.

White, Tony. *The Animator's Workbook*. New York: Watson-Guptill Publications, 1986.
This workbook is a complete course on drawing animated pictures.

PERIODICALS

Animation World Network Magazine
http://www.awn.com
Animation World Network is for anyone interested in breaking into the fields of animation or gaming, and contains articles, interviews, job listings, and more.

10

IN BETWEEN THE WORDS: GRAPHIC ARTIST

If you're like most people, you like information to involve images or visual aids. Sometimes words just aren't enough. Do you often look at graphics and think you could have done better than what you're shown? Do you love colors, designs, and art? If so, you may want to become a graphic artist. Graphic artists create the logos, buttons, and images that go on Web sites. A graphic artist may also create logos, images, and design the layout for printed brochures and publications.

Graphic artists are responsible for creating high-quality, professional-looking images for Web sites and print publications. They should have strong drawing and illustration skills and a good understanding of color and design. They need a sensitivity to the subject matter of each project. This means knowing just the right images and designs to use. Graphic artists must understand the goals of the company they are creating images for, as well as that company's customers. Their job is to create appealing images that attract customers to the company.

A graphic artist who works on the Web must also have knowledge of Web design and development. He or she may actually design Web pages, or he or she may create images for specific areas of a Web page. A Web graphic artist must understand elements that limit design options. This includes the fact that there are Web colors versus all the colors available. Image files should have small storage sizes so they can load over the Internet quickly.

Many graphic artists work on their own, as freelance artists or consultants. They create images and logos for many different businesses. They sell their services to Web development companies or media companies. Because of this, it is necessary for a graphic artist to maintain a

Some graphic artists use Pantone color fans and chips to choose palettes for the Web sites they help create.

portfolio of the best work that he or she has completed. He or she must be able to sell his or her services to many different small businesses and individuals.

Paying Your Dues

Many colleges offer two-year degrees in graphic art, which include Web design training. These are the candidates who will be looking for jobs in the same market as you. Fortunately, if you have a great portfolio, employers will overlook the lack of college experience. Graphic artist candidates should be creative and artistic, with the ability to draw and paint. Your portfolio will be used to prove this. Take art and drawing classes to learn basic design and color skills, and practice drawing for school or group projects. Save your best projects for your portfolio. Graphic artists must also be very familiar with the software and tools used in graphic arts and Web design. There are many books and classes on Adobe Photoshop and Macromedia Freehand, two of the most widely used tools. As an online graphic artist, you'll need to be familiar with Web design software such as Microsoft FrontPage or Macromedia Dreamweaver. You can even create an online portfolio, which shows your work as a graphic artist and Web artist.

Earning a Living

According to the U.S. Department of Labor, the average annual salary of a graphic artist is $36,680. Salaries range between $28,140 and $48,820. Graphic artists typically start at approximately $24,000 per year. Many graphic artists are freelancers. This means the salaries they make will vary on how much work they take on and how much they charge.It is best to check with local graphic artists working in your area to determine what the standard rate is, and set your own rates accordingly.

Where It Is Headed

According to the U.S. Department of Labor, employment of designers is expected to grow ten to twenty percent over the next six years. The Internet has created an entirely new medium for art and images, so there are many more jobs available in this field. Graphic artists stay on top of the latest tools and technologies by taking workshops. Graphic arts is an in-demand, stable field in which to find a career.

Creating Online Graphics

Graphic artists create many of the images, logos, and buttons that go on a Web site or printed publication to make it look attractive. When you browse through different Web sites, you'll notice that each site has its own unique look and feel, but you may not realize how many images have been created to make the site look as attractive as possible. Here is a list of just some of the images that graphic artists create:

- Logos are special symbols that companies use to identify their name in a unique and creative way.
- Buttons that say "Back," "Search," or "Send" appear throughout Web sites, and many are actually images with the same colors and style as the rest of the site.

This graphic artwork on BendableRubber.com helps to project the "zany fun" that the site's creator offers visitors.

- Background images provide the background for a Web page and are usually simple and subtle.
- Lines or dividers are used to divide sections of a Web page and may often be a color that matches the company's logo.
- Icons are small pictures that mean something to the user, such as a picture of a stop sign for the "Stop" button.
- Photographs and other high-quality images are usually limited on Web sites, as they take more time to download.

FOR MORE INFORMATION

ASSOCIATIONS

American Institute of Graphic Arts (AIGA)
164 Fifth Avenue
New York, NY 10010
(212) 807-1990
Web site: http://www.aiga.org
This is a professional association for design. According to its Web site, AIGA "supports the interests of professionals, educators and students who are engaged in the process of designing, regardless of where they are in the arc of their careers."

WEB SITES

CoolHomePages.com
http://www.coolhomepages.com
CoolHomePages.com is a Web site with links to hundreds of cool and attractive-looking sites, where designers can go to look for inspiration and great ideas.

Graphic Design Gate
http://www.graphicdesigngate.com
Graphic Design Gate provides lots of examples and resources for graphic artists and Web designers.

Guru.com
http://www.guru.com
Guru.com is a Web site where freelance artists and other freelance workers can go to find great jobs.

Web Developer's Journal
http://www.webdevelopersjournal.com

Web Developer's Journal provides helpful articles about creating a Web site and tools to download.

Web Style Guide

http://info.med.yale.edu/caim/manual

The Web Style Guide is a complete online style manual with information on interface, site and page design, graphics, multimedia, and animation.

BOOKS

Blatner, David, and Bruce Fraser. *Real World Photoshop 6.* Berkeley, CA: Peachpit Press, 2001.
This is a straightforward manual on using Photoshop 6.

Campbell, Alastair (Editor). *Digital Designers Bible.* New York: HarperCollins Publishers, 2005.
This informative rulebook is geared toward digital graphic artists.

Cohen, Sandee. *FreeHand 9 for Windows and Macintosh: Visual QuickStart Guide.* Berkeley, CA: Peachpit Press, 2000.
A step-by-step guide to using FreeHand 9, including information on creating GIF and JPEG graphics, controlling layouts, and creating graphics with Flash animation.

Douglas, Noel, Geert J. Strengholt, and Willem Velthoven. *Website Graphics Now: The Best of Global Site Design.* New York: Thames and Hudson, 1999.
This book describes current and future developments in the world of graphic arts.

Kelley, Tom, Jonathan Littman, and Tom Peters. *The Art of Innovation: Lessons in Creativity from Ideo, America's Leading Design Firm.* New York: Currency/Doubleday, 2001.
This book shows how the best ideas for products, logos, and brands are created.

Mohler, James. *Flash 5.0: Graphics, Animation and Interactivity.* Albany, NY: Delmar Thomson Learning, 2000.

COOL CAREERS WITHOUT COLLEGE

This straightforward guide to Flash 5 covers all of the latest features of Flash and offers exercises to practice what you've learned.

Niederst, Jennifer, and Richard Koman. *Learning Web Design: A Beginner's Guide to HTML, Graphics, and Beyond*. Sebastopol, CA: O'Reilly & Associates, 2001.
This book covers almost all topics related to Web design: HTML, graphics, and design. No previous knowledge of the Internet or Web design is necessary.

Pipes, Alan. *Production for Graphic Designers*. Upper Saddle River, NJ: Prentice Hall, 2005.
This book discusses the field of graphic art with coverage of Internet and online graphic art opportunities.

Stein, Bob. *Web Design Color Reference Card*. VisiBone, 2000.
This is a clear and logical reference card of colors for the World Wide Web.

Weinman, Lynda. *Designing Web Graphics.3*. Indianapolis, IN: New Riders Publishing, 1999.
This book addresses several topics related to creating graphics for the Web and provides information on the latest graphic design software.

Weinman, Lynda, and John Warren Lentz. *Deconstructing Web Graphics*. Indianapolis, IN: New Riders Publishing, 1998.
This book is filled with tips and useful information on graphic design software, graphic design, and Web development.

11

LET IT RIDE: DAY TRADER

Does the idea of using money to make money excite you? Do you spend time thinking or fantasizing about the finance industry and all its trends? If so, you may want to consider becoming a day trader. The excitement previously and exclusively reserved for Wall Street can now be accessed by

The trading floor of the New York Stock Exchange

anyone in the world through the Internet. Day traders buy and sell stock and other securities in order to make a profit. They use the Internet to make money for themselves and their clients.

Online brokerage firms such as E*TRADE and Ameritrade are available to facilitate trading. Day traders first develop a plan or strategy to make a profit from the stocks they buy and sell. They spend time on the World Wide Web, researching companies and stocks. They look for the best purchases available. They buy the stocks, and then sell the stocks when the price rises, so they make a profit. Day traders do all this within the same market day. They start the whole process over again the next day, with new stocks and securities. Traders must be dedicated and hardworking, and must be farsighted enough to work through difficult times and big losses. This is because stock market prices can vary greatly by the minute, and clients can lose a lot of money by the minute as well.

Traders can be freelancers working for themselves, or employed at companies such as trading firms. A firm has clients who give their money to the firm for trading. The firm will usually guide the trader as to which types of stocks to purchase and what strategies to use. Many trading firms have elaborate training programs for their employees. Traders are taught the exact methods and strategies to use when trading with the company's, or clients', money.

Traders who work for a trading firm often use their own money to trade with as well, especially as they learn the ups and downs of the stock market. This can either be very worthwhile, or a grim disappointment, depending on the success or failure of each trade.

Paying Your Dues

Colleges offer degrees in finance, and these are the candidates you'll be competing with for jobs. In order to be

competitive, you should learn about the stock market: how it works, how to get started, and what factors affect stock prices. You can also test your instincts by watching stock prices throughout the day. Pretend that you bought stocks, and calculate how much you made or lost depending on when you would sell throughout the day.

There are many books and Web sites with information about getting started in the stock market. Visit your school and local libraries and read up on day trading techniques. A day trader must be quick and resourceful on the Internet. A lot of time is spent investigating companies and trends.

Earning a Living

There is no set salary for day traders. Those who work on their own, using their own money actually play a part in determining what their salary will be. If they make money, then their salary is large, but if they lose money, then they lose their salary as well. A day trader must be disciplined and restrained so that he or she does not lose all of his or her money.

Day traders employed at firms work on a commission and earn a percentage of what their trading earns, so they

The headquarters of the National Association of Securities Dealers Automated Quotation System, or NASDAQ, is located in New York City. NASDAQ was the world's first electronic stock market.

don't have as much risk as day traders who work for themselves. The trick to survival is having backup funds.

Where It Is Headed

Day trading courses, workshops, and schools are increasing, because more working professionals dream of making profits off the stock market. They keep their day jobs, and trade with their earnings. While this is alluring, many of these professionals learn it is best to leave it up to the professional traders who dedicate their life to the job, and really know what they're doing.

Trading Things Unseen

Securities, the items that are usually bought and sold by day traders, are new and interesting concepts to many people. Here is a list of items that may be traded:

A stock is a small piece of ownership in a company. Stocks are more valuable when a company makes money than when a company doesn't make money.

A bond is a loan from the owner of the bond to a company or to the government. Government bonds are usually very secure, while corporate (or company) bonds are less secure.

A mutual fund is a professionally managed set of stocks and other securities. Individuals or companies can buy a small portion of a mutual fund, instead of buying just one or two stocks.

An option is the right to buy or sell a stock at a specific price. Options are often traded or given to long-term employees as benefits.

FOR MORE INFORMATION

WEB SITES

About.com Day Trading
http://daytrading.about.com/?once=true&
This informative site explains the life and work of day traders.

CNN Financial Network
http://money.cnn.com
CNN Financial Network provides up-to-the-minute news on the markets, companies, funds, and trading strategies, as well as tools, links, and resources useful for anyone in the business world.

Datek Online—Ameritrade
http://www.datek.com
Datek is an online brokerage firm popular for their one-low-fee-for-trades pricing structure. They also offer free real-time streaming quotes for their customers, as well as an online learning center.

Day Trading Online
http://www.daytradingonline.com
Day Trading Online is an online source for instruction, training, and tools for day traders.

E*TRADE Financial
http://www.etrade.com
E*TRADE, a well-known online brokerage firm, offers a number of benefits to its customers, including low trading fees, options, short and margin trading, after hours trading, and real-time quotes.

The Motley Fool
http://www.fool.com
The Motley Fool is a useful resource for stock quotes, news, strategies, and research, and it provides a free beginner's guide to the stock market.

MSN MoneyCentral Stock Screener
http://moneycentral.msn.com/investor/finder/predefstocks.asp
MSN's MoneyCentral Stock Screener is a great tool for searching for specific stocks, with predefined searches built in, as well as the ability to create custom-defined stock searches.

Online Trading Academy
http://www.tradingacademy.com
OTA offers online training programs in trading and investing.

TheStreet.com
http://www.thestreet.com
TheStreet.com provides articles, news, and analysis, plus quotes, financial calculators, metrics, special reports, and a financial terms glossary.

BOOKS

Baird, Bob, and Craig McBurney. *Electronic Day Trading to Win*. New York: John Wiley & Sons, 1999.
This book covers all aspects of day trading, including its history, a typical trading day, and how to choose the best stocks.

Douglas, Mark. *Trading in the Zone: Master the Market with Confidence, Discipline, and a Winning Attitude*. New York: New York Institute of Finance, 2000.
This book details a popular strategy that takes into account the discipline, confidence, and attitude of the trader.

Fontanills, George A., and Tom Gentile. *The Stock Market Course*. New York: John Wiley & Sons, 2000.
The Stock Market Course is a step-by-step course for beginners who want to learn the basic rules and terms used in the stock market.

Griffis, Michael and Lita Epstein. *Trading for Dummies.* Hoboken, NJ: John Wiley & Sons, Inc., 2004.
This is a how-to book on stock market trading.

Patel, Alpesh B. *Net-trading: Strategies from the Frontiers of Electronic Day Trading.* Upper Saddle River, NJ: Financial Times Prentice Hall Publishing, 2000.
This book describes and explains several of the most popular strategies of day traders.

Sindell, Kathleen. *Investing Online for Dummies*. Hoboken, NJ: John Wiley & Sons, Inc., 2005.
This book describes and explains online trading in friendly, informal language.

Sarkovich, Misha T. *Electronic Day Trading Made Easy: Become a Successful Trader*. Roseville, CA: Prima Publishing, 2000.
This is an insightful and instructive guide to the basics of successful day trading for beginners as well as experienced traders.

Turner, Michael P. *Day Trading into the Millennium*. Austin, TX: Traders Resource, 1998.
This book presents several strategies and ideas for day trading based on the history of the markets and real-life trading experience.

Turner, Toni. *A Beginner's Guide to Day Trading Online*. Holbrook, MA: Adams Media Corporation, 2000.
This book contains sound, real-world trading advice and ideas in an easy-to-understand format.

PERIODICALS

Fast Company
http://www.fastcompany.com
This magazine is full of new and innovative approaches to the business world, for "how smart people work."

12

PAID TO PLAY: GAME TESTER

Can you imagine being paid for your opinions about a video game? Can you see yourself playing all sorts of video games, not just for fun but to earn a living? Are you an ace at finding the tricks and secrets in games? If so, you may want to consider being a game tester. A game tester usually starts working on a game before it actually *is* a game.

He or she may review the idea to determine if it will be a good, entertaining, playable game. As a game is being developed, the tester will check the graphics to make sure that they are correct, understandable, and of good quality. He or she will play the game to test for obvious errors or glitches. The tester will then report back to the programmers exactly where each error occurs and under what exact conditions.

As development of the game progresses, the game tester will look for smaller and less obvious errors. He or she will have to play the game repeatedly, working through all scenarios. He or she plays through all different levels of the game and every different possibility, making sure that every last detail has been looked at and every possible error solved. Sometimes a game tester will work very long hours, especially right before a new game is to be released, making sure every bug is fixed.

Game testers need strong analysis skills, be good at writing and communicating about errors in the programs, and have a passion for playing and evaluating video games.

Paying Your Dues

Currently, there are no degrees awarded for being a game tester. There are classes, however, and in the future, degrees will be offered for Quality Assurance. Quality Assurance is another term for game and software testing. This means

Game testers' jobs involve more than just playing games. They must provide detailed analysis, which require strong troubleshooting and communication skills.

you'll want to come into the field with experience and proven skill in order to be competitive. Testers must be familiar with video games: how they work, how they should work, secrets of the games, and problems with the games. They should be able to analyze many different scenarios and come up with solutions when needed. They should be able to do this quickly and efficiently, as companies won't want to pay someone who takes forever to test a game. Read books, visit Web sites, and take classes that teach the secrets of video games.

Future game testers should become familiar with the technology behind making the games, such as programming and design. This will help them understand and communicate errors to the programmers and designers.

Earning a Living

According to Gignews.com, temporarily staffed testers make between $6.50 and $8.00 per hour. Permanenty staffed game testers earn between $7 and $15 per hour, or between $15,000 and $30,000 per year. Some companies are often willing to hire teenagers still in high school or just out of high school.

Experienced and highly talented game testers can earn much more. In addition, many game testers go on to become game developers, artists, or testing managers, which usually have higher salaries.

Where It Is Headed

There are many more people who wish they were game testers than there are opportunities for game testers. However, game testing is a necessary and useful job, and nearly every company that creates and sells video games needs testers. So long as there is a desire and use for video games, there will be a need for humans to test them.

Thumbs Up, Thumbs Down: Game Testing

Game testing has its good and bad points. Here are some of the pros and cons of being a game tester:

Thumbs Up:
- You get to play video games all day and get paid for it!
- You get to give your opinion about how a game should work.
- You may get free games to take home.
- You'll be finding out about new games before they hit the market.

Thumbs Down:
- You have to play a game over and over again, which can make a game boring after much repetition.
- You may have to work long hours, especially right before a game is released.
- Jobs may be competitive and difficult to find.
- Pay is low in the beginning of your career, and you may need another job while testing to make ends meet.

FOR MORE INFORMATION

ASSOCIATIONS

International Game Developers Association
600 Harrison Street
San Francisco, CA 94107
(415) 947-6235
Web site: http://www.igda.org
The International Game Developers Association is a nonprofit organization for developers of games and entertainment software. Members receive free or discounted rates on publications, conferences, and software.

WEB SITES

GameDev.net
http://www.gamedev.net
GameDev.net is a Web site for developers and others in the video game industry, and it contains articles, resources, job listings, and chat rooms.

GameJobs.com
http://www.gamejobs.com
This Web site is a job board for those looking to work in the computer and video gaming industry. It also has tips, links, and resource materials.

GigNews.com
http://www.gignews.com
This Web site features news, tutorials, inside information, and job listings for anyone in the computer game industry.

Monster.com
http://www.monster.com
Monster.com is a popular job-search site for all types of careers. It's a great place to find game testing and development careers.

BOOKS

Adams, Ernest. *Break into the Game Industry: How to Get a Job Making Video Games (Career Series)*. New York: McGraw-Hill, 2003.
This book explains how games are built and published, as well as how to land a job as a tester.

Asakura, Reiji. *Revolutionaries at Sony: The Making of the Sony PlayStation and the Visionaries Who Conquered the World of Video Games*. New York: McGraw-Hill, 2000.
An interesting look at how Sony broke into the video game industry and created the world's top-selling game machine, the PlayStation.

DeLoura, Mark. *Game Programming Gems II*. Hingham, MA: Charles River Media, 2001.
This book provides solutions and ideas for programming games.

Gershenfeld, Alan and Cecilia Barajas, Mark Loparco. *Game Plan: The Insider's Guide to Breaking In and Succeeding in the Computer and Video Game Business*. New York: St. Martin's Press, 2003.
This book provides a comprehensive look at the gaming industry, and how-to suggestions on breaking into the business.

Jones, George. *Gaming 101: A Contemporary History of PC and Video Games*. Plano, TX: Wordware Publishing, Inc., 2005.
This book describes the companies, games, people, and business strategies behind the video gaming industry.

Kent, Steven L. *The First Quarter: A 25-year History of Video Games*. Marietta, OH: BWD Press, 2000.
This book provides an insider's look at the history of video games, as well as the people behind some of the most popular video games ever created.

Mohler, James. *Flash 5.0: Graphics, Animation and Interactivity*. Albany, NY: Delmar Thomson Learning, 2000.
This straightforward guide to Flash 5 covers all of the latest features of Flash and offers exercises to practice what you've learned.

Rouse, Richard. *Game Design: Theory and Practice*. Plano, TX: Wordware Publishing, 2000.
This book discusses game design topics such as adventure, storytelling, player motivations, testing, and has information on all types of computer games.

Saltzman, Marc. *Game Design: Secret of the Sages*. Indianapolis, IN: Brady Games, 1999.
This text provides information about the gaming industry, as well as theories and insights on game design, from experts in the field.

Sheff, David, and Andy Eddy. *Game Over Press Start to Continue*. Wilton, CT: GamePress, 1999.
This is an insider's look into what it takes to succeed in today's computer game industry.

PERIODICALS

Animation World Network Magazine
http://www.awn.com
Animation World is for anyone interested in getting into the fields of animation or gaming, and contains articles, interviews, job listings, and more.

13

ON THE HUNT: ONLINE RESEARCHER

Have you ever looked for facts and figures on the Web? Are you able to find information on just about anything you're looking for on the Internet? If you love sorting through facts and figures to come up with just the right thing, you could become an online researcher. Online researchers work for themselve or for employers. The

Keep Me Posted

About FIND/SVP

Search

Find it Fast ▶

researcher may gather information about people, companies, or competitors. He or she may check facts to determine their truth and validity.

Online researchers spend a great deal of time surfing the Web. They must be curious and interested in gathering information or digging up details. They must possess the ability to find what they want on the Internet. They need to be very familiar with the best search engines and tools. The Internet is full of various sites. A researcher has to know which ones are reliable and which are not.

Some online researchers may compile lists of people or companies who match certain criteria. For example, many companies and technical recruiters hire online researchers to search for online resumés. A company may hire an online researcher to compile a list of potential customers.

Other online researchers check facts and data to verify their validity. Before printing information in an article, a media company may hire an online researcher to determine if certain facts are true. A production company may have an online researcher check dates and times before it produces a historical movie.

Online researchers must be able to stay focused on one task for long periods at a time. They must have the determination and skills to find the information that they're looking for, even when it is proving difficult. They need the ability to realize when the information simply isn't available. Online

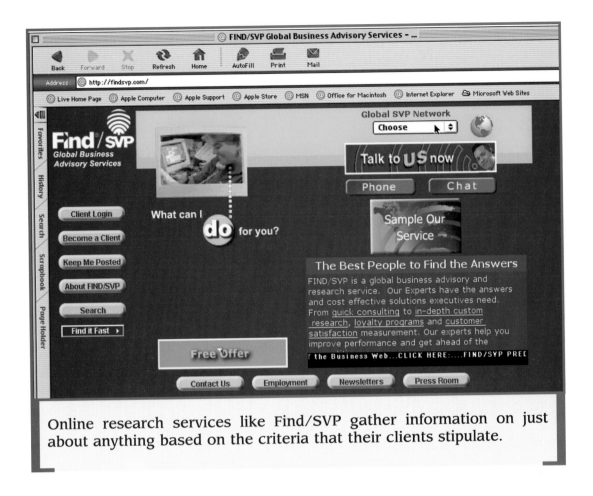

Online research services like Find/SVP gather information on just about anything based on the criteria that their clients stipulate.

research is a little like detective work. You look for clues to help you solve a puzzle and find the information you need.

Paying Your Dues

Like the other careers in this book, you don't need a college degree to be an online researcher. You'll need to be very familiar with the Internet and able to get around in search engines and informational sites quickly and easily. You should know how to use advanced searches on search engines. A course on the ins and outs of the Internet is

Making a historical movie like *Pearl Harbor* requires a lot of research.

highly recommended for getting started in this career. Courses dealing with finding people, information, and facts online are also useful, as are private detective courses. Libraries offer classes on using the Internet and other electronic sources for fact checking.

Earning a Living

Online researchers generally earn between $24,000 and $30,000 per year. Often, they earn an hourly wage ($12 to $15 per hour) or a payment for each piece of information they collect. For example, a nonprofit organization such as a museum needs funds. They often get these funds from individual donations. The museum would hire an online researcher to compile a list of wealthy people who donate to the arts. The researcher would be paid for each new contact he or she finds for the list. He or she could also be paid an hourly wage or a flat fee.

Many online researchers work at home, doing contract jobs for several different companies. This allows them to work as much or as little as they choose. This is an ideal job for someone who would prefer to work from home, on his or her own schedule.

Where It Is Headed

The field of online research is a relatively new one. Many companies are just beginning to see the benefits of hiring online researchers, and the job descriptions are usually somewhat varied. As more information becomes available online, online researchers will be able to do more and will become more marketable. It is important to realize that this is a field that will grow and change in the future, so it is better for those who are willing to be flexible along their career path.

Searching in the Binary World

An online researcher must be very familiar with search engines and know how to perform advanced searches online. Most search engines allow you to enter keywords, as well as logical words, to help you find exactly what you need. Here are some tips on using advanced search engines:

- A keyword is a word that will produce results that are related to your topic.
- The word "and" is placed in between two keywords when you would like to search for both words.
- The word "or" is placed in between two keywords when you would like to search for either word.
- The word "not" is placed in front of a keyword that you do not wish to include in your search.

Most search engines have a help page that explains their advanced search capabilities. Check the search engine's help page to learn more about its advanced search.

FOR MORE INFORMATION

WEB SITES

Guru.com
http://www.guru.com
Guru.com is a Web site where freelance workers can go to find great jobs. This site often has a number of unique or cutting edge jobs, such as those in online research.

Google.com
http://www.google.com
Google.com has become one of the largest, most comprehensive search engines in the world. Researchers can also use search options such as "images" to find photographs.

Mamma.com
http://www.mamma.com
Mamma.com is an online search tool that allows users to search several of the major search engines at once.

Monster.com
http://www.monster.com
Monster.com is a popular job-search site for all types of careers. It's a great place to find online research careers.

Northern Light
http://www.northernlight.com
This search engine links to more sites than most and uses special search software to help users find exactly what they're looking for faster and easier than many other search engines.

Yahoo!
http://www.yahoo.com
Yahoo!, one of the Web's most popular and easy-to-use search engines, contains links to thousands of Web sites and Web pages around the world.

BOOKS

Basch, Reva, and Mary Ellen Bates. *Researching Online for Dummies.* Foster City, CA: IDG Books Worldwide, Inc., 2000.
This is beginner's guide to online research, this book covers specialty search engines, catalogs, reference sites, online libraries, and more.

Basch, Reva, Mary E. Bates, and Howard Rheingold. *Secrets of the Super Net Searchers: The Reflections, Revelations, and Hard-Won Wisdom of 35 of the World's Top Internet Researchers.* Wilton, CT: Pemberton Press, 1996.
This book contains insights, tips, and techniques by experts in searching and finding information on the Internet.

Berkman, Robert I. *Find It Fast: How to Uncover Expert Information on Any Subject Online or in Print.* New York: Harper Resource, 2000.
This book will tell you, step-by-step, how to track down any type of information you may be looking for.

Butler, John A. *Cybersearch: Research Techniques in the Electronic Age.* New York: Penguin Reference, 1998.
This easy-to-understand reference guide includes information on Internet resources, public access catalogs, news groups, and more.

Friedman, Barbara G. *Web Search Savvy: Strategies and Shortcuts for Online Research.* Mahwah, NJ: Lawrence Erlbaum Associates, Inc., 2004.
This book is geared toward students and researchers. It shows how to get the most out of search engines and other online resources.

Gralla, Preston. *How the Internet Works*. Indianapolis, IN: Que, 2001.
This book provides explanations and information about aspects of the Internet that most people find confusing, including explanations on Web browsers, e-mail, search engines, multimedia, and more.

Pack, Thomas. *10 Minute Guide to Business Research on the Net.* Indianapolis, IN: Que, 1997.
An easy-to-learn, step-by-step approach to doing research for your business on the Internet.

Rowlands, Robin. *Creative Guide to Research: How to Find What You Need . . . Online or Offline.* Franklin Lakes, NJ: Career Press, Incorporated, 2000.
This book discusses how research can be a fun adventure. It gives in-depth advice for researching online and offline.

Schlein, Alan M. and Peter J. Weber (Editor). *Find It Online: The Complete Guide to Online Research.* Tempe, AZ: BRB Publications, Inc., 2004.
A useful and handy resource guide for help in finding anything on the Internet.

14

ONLINE AND AROUND THE WORLD: TRAVEL AGENT

With just a few clicks of the keyboard, an entire family is set to visit Rome. Thanks to the Web, those clicks can be made a world away, such as Kansas. The person in charge of arranging the details of the trip—hotel reservations, transportation, dinner plans, special entertainment—is the travel agent. If you are interested in travel, love to work with people, and are very good with details, you may want to consider becoming a travel agent.

Travel agents usually work in a travel agency. They have a computer system that allows them to book airline, hotel, and other reservations for their clients at the touch of a button. Travel agents research the Internet to find out what's going on in a location where his or her client wants to travel. Travel agents know the best ways to get quality travel for low prices. They also know about resorts because many resorts offer travel trips to agents. This is so that the agents can recommend places they have actually visited to their clients.

Corporate travel agents work with customers who travel for business. Their needs are often different from the needs of those who travel for leisure. For example, a client traveling for business will want to follow his or her schedule closely. He or she will be more concerned with a good hotel and transportation than with local attractions. Business travelers are usually less concerned about budget and more concerned about comfort and time. Travel agents must understand the various needs of their customers in order to serve them better. They must be friendly and have strong communication skills.

Agents must be good with computers, organized, and detail oriented. They need to make sure that dates, times, and prices are accurate. Most travel agents also love to travel and bring that love of travel to their customers.

Paying Your Dues

There are many agents in the industry who don't have college degrees. In order to be successful in the career, you'll need computer and people skills. There are many travel agent schools that provide basic training. These schools teach geography, sales and marketing, and travel industry procedures. They also teach students about the computer systems used by travel agents. If there is no travel agent school in your area, it is possible to take a correspondence course.

After completing one of these programs, you should take the Travel Agent Proficiency (TAP) exam. This test measures basic relevant knowledge and will help you get your first job as a travel agent.

Earning a Living

According to the U.S. Department of Labor, travel agents earn between $20,800 and $33,580 per year. Most travel agents start at about $20,000 per year. Travel agents may also earn a commission, or a percentage of all of the travel that they sell. This means that their salary will vary, depending on the amount of travel that they sell. The average salary for a corporate travel manager is $65,000.

Travel agents must be able to describe the activities involved in specialized travel packages, such as this horse-riding tour of the Grand Canyon.

Travel agents often post pictures of vacation spots on their Web sites.

Where It Is Headed

Even though people can book their own trips through the Internet, agents are still a preferred choice. According to the American Society of Travel Agents, travel agents book eighty-seven percent of cruises, and eighty-one percent of all tours and packages. They book fifty-one percent of all airline tickets, and forty-seven percent of all hotels. They even book forty-five percent of all car rentals. Business travelers will continue to use agents because it makes their schedules easier. They don't have time to search through the Web for the best prices. They pay a travel agent to do it for them.

According to the Travel Industry Association of America, travel in the United States has increased over the past several years and is expected to continue increasing. This means that there will be a continued need for agents in the future.

Travel and Tourism: Fast Facts

- Travel and tourism is the largest industry, employer, and foreign-revenue earner in the United States.
- Over 18 million people work in the travel industry in the United States.
- Beaches are the leading tourist destination in the United States.
- Americans take about one billion trips each year.

FOR MORE INFORMATION

ASSOCIATIONS

American Society of Travel Agents
1101 King Street, Suite 200
Alexandria, VA 22314
(703) 739-2782
Web site: http://www.astanet.com
ASTA is the world's oldest and largest organization of travel professionals throughout the world.

WEB SITES

About.com Budget Travel Guide
http://budgettravel.about.com
All about budget travel, this guide provides insights and tips on getting the most bang for your travel buck.

Become a Travel Agent
http://www.becomeatravelagent.com
This Web site provides information and links to anyone interested in becoming a travel agent.

Great American Outdoor Pages (Gorp)

http://www.gorp.com
The Great American Outdoor Pages site contains information on outdoor and adventure vacation packages.

HotelGuide.com
http://www.hotelguide.com
HotelGuide.com lists thousands of different hotels in cities throughout

the world. Very useful for finding the perfect hotel in major cities as well as out-of-the-way locations.

Monster.com
http://www.monster.com
Monster.com is a popular job-search site for all types of careers. It's a great place to find travel agent positions.

TravelDazzle.com
http://www.traveldazzle.com
TravelDazzle.com is a Web site with information and prices for hundreds of unique and interesting tours and vacation packages. Useful for finding the perfect vacation for yourself or your clients.

BOOKS

Evenson, Renee. *Customer Service 101: Basic Lessons to Be Your Best*. Whitehouse Station, NJ: Bull's Eye Publishing, 1997.
This title clearly explains the basic rules for great customer service and is useful for anyone in the service industry, including travel agents.

Fanning, Patrick, Matthew McKay, and Martha Davis. *Messages: The Communication Skills Book*. Oakland, CA: New Harbinger Publications, 1995.
This book shows how to master communication in personal and professional life and is a must-have for anyone in a service industry, as well as for those interested in enhancing their lives through communication.

Mancini, Marc. *Access: Introduction to Hospitality and Tourism*. Florence, KY: Thomson Delmar Learning, 2004.
This book provides information about the travel industry, as well as discussing all of the major brands used in travel.

Monaghan, Kelly. *Home-Based Travel Agent: How to Succeed in Your Own Travel Marketing Business*. Branford, CT: Intrepid Traveler, 2001.
This book describes how to set up a travel agency from home, with

information on researching trips, getting customers, and maximizing profits.

Ogg, Tom, and Joanie Ogg. *How to Start a Home Based Travel Agency*. Valley Center, CA: Ogg Tom & Associates, 1997.
A clear and complete book, it illustrates how to start a home-based travel agency.

Payette, Douglas A. *So You Want to Be a Travel Agent: An Introduction to Domestic Travel*. Englewood Cliffs, NJ: Prentice Hall, 1995.
This text is a basic introduction to the travel industry, with information on everything from customer service to travel agent perks and benefits.

Raza, Ivo. *Heads in Beds: Hospitality and Tourism Marketing*. Upper Saddle River, NJ: Prentice Hall, 2004.
This book covers the business and marketing side of travel agencies.

Todd, Ginger, and Susan Rice. *Travel Perspectives: A Guide to Becoming a Travel Agent*. Albany, NY: Delmar Thomson Learning, 2001.
This book covers every aspect of the travel industry, from air travel to tours and cruises, and is ideal for those beginning a career in travel.

PERIODICALS

Travel and Leisure
Web site: http://www.travelandleisure.com
This travel magazine provides helpful insight into destinations, vacation packages, and issues within the travel industry.

CORRESPONDENCE COURSE

Thomson Delmar Learning
(800) 347-7707
Web site: http://www.hospitality-tourism.delmar.com
This center for travel education offers training as well as a home-study program.

GLOSSARY

blog Short for Weblog or Web log, an online journal.

commission Percentage of the money received during a business deal.

distance learning Education that takes place outside a classroom, such as through the use of videotapes or the Internet.

e-commerce Business that is conducted through electronic means, especially the Internet.

HTML (hypertext markup language) Programming code used to create a Web site.

Internet Global network connecting millions of computers.

ISP (Internet service provider) Company that provides Internet service to companies and individuals.

Java Programming language designed to develop applications for the Internet.

search engine Program that gathers information from sites on the World Wide Web.

stock Small portion of ownership in a company.

virtual Something that is created or simulated by a computer.

INDEX

About the Author

Tonya Buell is the founder and CEO of TravelDazzle.com, an online travel and tour directory. She has also worked on numerous Web sites as a freelancer and while employed at the Web design firm Razorfish. This is her second book about careers in the Web industry.

Photo Credits

Cover © Norbert von der Groeben/The Image Works; pp. 9, 11 © Vincent Hobbs/SuperStock; p. 14 © Pictor; pp. 18, 20 © Pictor; p. 22 © John Bazemore/AP Wide World; pp. 27, 29 © Pictor; p. 31 © Stuart Ranson/AP Wide World; pp. 37, 40 © Frank Siteman/Index Stock Imagery; pp. 46, 49 © Grandpix/Index Stock Imagery; pp. 50, 60 © Eyewire; p. 51 © SuperStock; pp. 56, 58 © Francisco Cruz/SuperStock; pp. 66, 69 © PhotoDisc; pp. 75, 78 © Noble Desktop; pp. 84, 86, 94, 96 by Cindy Reiman; pp. 88, 124 © The Everett Collection; p. 99 © Bendablerubber.com by Aaron Stewart; pp. 103, 106 © Reuters NewMedia Inc./Corbis; p. 104 © Charles Orrico/SuperStock; pp. 113, 115 © SCEA, Bob Riha Jr., HO/AP Wide World; pp. 121, 123 © Find/SVP; pp. 130, 134 © Mark Newman/SuperStock; p. 133 © Steve Vidler/SuperStock.